Rebuilding Muslim Nations

L. Ali Khan

Founder, Legal Scholar Academy
Professor of Law, Washburn University

DEDICATION

This book is dedicated to Muslim intellectuals, lawyers,
jurists, judges, politicians, generals, journalists, poets,
students, and social critics who are making huge efforts to
rebuild Muslim nations.

.

Table of Contents

PREFACE

This book offers critical assessments of Muslim nations and communities, offering insights for rebuilding political and social institutions. Pakistan is the focus of this book. Other countries examined are Iran, Bangladesh, and Arab nations from Saudi Arabia to Tunisia. A few chapters explore the role of Western intellectuals and politicians in waging battles against Islamic civilization.

Three broad realities emerge from these critical assessments. First, Muslim communities are unable to construct durable and accountable institutions. There is a tendency among ruling elites to see law as a barrier and rotation of power as a lawless contest. Fair elections are rarely held and results of elections are rarely accepted by losers. The electoral system is frequently corrupt, incompetent, and designed to preserve the hegemony of familial political parties.

Furthermore, some Muslim nations, particularly in the Arab Middle East, argue against the establishment of answerable democracy. Arab communities themselves are skeptical of democracy as a preferred form of government. Kingships, Amirdoms, military dictatorships, and family monopolies occupy the political scene in most Arab countries. These structures may furnish social stability but the people feel excluded and alienated. Theocratic democracy in Iran is limited in scope as candidates for elections are screened and excluded if the Council of Guardians rejects their religious credentials.

Muslim nations need not embrace liberal democracy founded on secularism, individual rights, and the Lockean concept of property. Yet, political structures unresponsive to the will of the people are inherently depressing and detrimental to creative energies. Political and social freedom is necessary for individual and communitarian creativity. However, mob democracy is as detrimental to a safe society as are unresponsive political institutions.

Second, widespread violence across Muslim communities is tearing apart their social and economic fabric. Violence is perpetrated in the name of takfirization, declaring others to be non-Muslims or anti-Islam. Sunni groups believe that Shia communities have deviated from true teachings of Islam. This type of violence is godfathered by some Arab nations for geopolitical reasons. Unfortunately, Iran-Saudi Arabia cold war for regional leadership contributes to Shia-Sunni conflict. Takfirization is also a cause for violence against Sufi shrines as some militant groups believe that Sufis corrupt the purity of the Shariah and misguide followers of Islam. Unless Muslim communities reclaim diversity as a premium Islamic value in matters of faith, religious violence will continue to disrupt normal life and social harmony.

Third, Muslim communities are showing unprecedented intolerance against non-Muslims. While Muslim immigrants enjoy religious freedom in European and North American countries, religious minorities, including Christians and Hindus, are under attack in predominantly Muslim nations. Churches are burnt. Individuals are falsely accused of defaming the Prophet of Islam. To make matters worse, some Western politicians, artists, and academics also provoke Muslims by defaming Islam, offering nonsensical research to argue that the Qur'an was fabricated, and drawing cartoons of the Prophet.

Time has come to rethink. Muslims need to rebuild their communities by instituting three major reforms. One, they must construct constitutional political institutions founded on the will of the people. Second, they must shun violence as a means of dispute resolution. Third, they must repudiate all forms of takfirization, declaring others to be non-Muslims or anti-Islam. Muslims must show respect for diverse religious beliefs within and without Islam.

1. MUSLIM DICTATORS

The dictators of the Middle East have a morbid love affair with power; they are prepared to do any harm to maintain power; they do not easily relinquish power; and, they, arising from the core of the Muslim world, disgrace the religion of Islam, forcing non-Muslims to conclude that it must be Islam that prompts rulers to forcibly establish sole proprietorships. In the eighteenth century, Montesquieu branded the Muslim Middle East as an incorrigible land of despots. The most recent arrogation of dictatorial powers is underway in Egypt where President Muhammad Morsi, holding unimpeachable Islamic credentials, has allegedly assumed Pharaoh's powers, frustrating judges, intellectuals, and the ordinary people who sacrificed liberty and life in overthrowing Hosni Mubarak, a secular self-seeker, who ruled Egypt with an iron fist for nearly 30 years.

It is not only Egypt that produces despots. It is the entire Arab region stretching from Morocco to Bahrain. In Libya, Colonel Muammar Gaddafi, the son of a poverty-stricken Bedouin, seized power in a military coup in 1969. Forgetting his humble roots, Gaddafi established a self-glorifying dictatorship that lasted for over 40 years. In Iraq, Saddam Hussein used every means necessary, including chemical weapons against the Kurds, to retain power. In Tunisia and Yemen, the people endured lengthy dictatorships. In Syria, Bashar Assad, a physician by profession, has brought untold suffering to his people but shows little remorse and no intention of leaving the reign of power. The Gulf States have established hereditary fiefdoms, equipped and willing to crush opposition with merciless machinery. Whether the ruler is Shia or Sunni, Bedouin or physician, military or civilian, secular or religious, whoever assumes power in the Arab region turns into a ghastly and irremovable dictator.

It Is Not Islam

It is wrong to blame the religion of Islam as a source of Arab despotism. Islam is compatible with various forms of government but under no circumstances does Islam allow the absolute reign of a single individual, single family, single race, or single sect. In fact, it is inaccurate to associate Islam with Arabs. Islam, though it originated in Mecca and Medina, has never been confined to the Arab region. The Arabic-speaking Muslims constitute only one-sixth of the world Muslim population. Furthermore, not all Arabs are Muslims. Even the definition of who is an Arab is controversial because the Egyptians, for example, though they speak Arabic, are not Arabs. The Arab region is actually an Arabic-speaking region. The Arab League, an international organization of 22 Arab states, indeed a congregation of despots and hereditary rulers, who often dislike each other, fantasize Arab unity rather than Muslim unity in the world.

While the Arab region tramples over the will of the people, prominent states in the rest of the Muslim world are emerging as democracies. Turkey and Iran, the most prominent countries in the Middle East, are experimenting with democracy at the opposite ends of Islamic ethos.

Turkey, a secular state, after successfully suppressing military interventions, has broadened the democratic base to allow Islamic parties to participate in general elections. Iran, a theocratic democracy, screens candidates who can run for office, thus maintaining the hold of the Shia clergy. And yet, the Iranian constitution allows no single person, not even the Leader, a religious office reserved for the Chief Ayatollah, to exercise unlimited powers. The Iranian presidency is limited to two terms.

Further away from the Arab region, the Muslim world has little forbearance for dictators. Pakistan, a country made in the name of Islam, offers the most extensive political liberty, allowing all political parties, ranging from religious fundamentalists to communists, to organize and contest federal and provincial elections. Periodically, military generals interrupt the democratic process but no military ruler has been able to survive more than ten years in office. Malaysia, a state highly innovative in Islamic financing, and Indonesia, the largest Muslim nation in the world, are fusing democracy with the teachings of Islam. By contrast, the Arab region, despite the struggle and sacrifice of poets, intellectuals, and the people, cannot shake off the unrepresentative forms of government.

Anti-Heroism

There are numerous reasons why the Arab region produces irremovable and ugly despots, many prepared to kill their own citizens. In this section, I will argue that the Arab region should abandon hero-worship, an element deeply entrenched in the Arab culture, as it has been in the Italian culture, a comparison that Thomas Carlyle made with admiration but failed to realize that heroism leads to fascism. To combat despotism, the people of the Arab region need to deliberatively cultivate anti-heroism, a new cultural belief that considers all rulers as potentially abusive and secretively evil. This political cynicism, though it might not always be accurate, is critical for warding off despots.

3

As a general principle, a nation must be anti-hero if it wants to establish enduring democracy. Unfortunately, a nation that looks for great heroes ends up with ugly dictators.

The most practical way of legislating anti-heroism is not to permit any ruler to stay in power for more than ten years, preferably less. "No person shall be elected to the office of the President more than twice" are the priceless words of the 22nd amendment to the U.S. Constitution. Those who loved Ronald Reagan as a hero wished to repeal the 22nd amendment so that Reagan could run for a third term. Thankfully, several attempts to repeal the 22nd amendment have failed.

In addition to law, an anti-hero culture preempts dictatorships. It is no surprise that India and the United States are the most successful democracies in the world. This is so because their people rarely see present and future rulers as infallible heroes; they see rulers as necessary evil for running state affairs; and, they have little doubt that politicians are mostly self-seekers, persons in search of power and personal glory. With rare exceptions, almost every leader's soul is fouled as soon as the leader becomes the ruler. In 1887, British historian John Acton put it well: "Power tends to corrupt, and absolute power corrupts absolutely. Great men are almost always bad man." This conviction lies at the heart of anti-hero cultures.

The Arab culture, which has greatly contributed to the world civilization, may continue to adore leaders but it must reconsider hero-worship. The people must compel rulers, under law, to leave office after an appointed term. When rulers know that they must become ordinary citizens again, their abuse of power is limited. When rulers are ordinary persons, ordinary persons can aspire to become rulers. This wisdom defines the authenticity of universal democracy. George Bernard Shaw put it aptly that "the pursuit of the superhuman" leads to "indiscriminate contempt for the human." Even more strongly, the Quran warns the peoples of the world, not just Muslims, to reject rulers who extol themselves as mighty saviors. "And Pharaoh issued a call to his people, saying, "O my people! Does not the dominion over Egypt belong to me, as all these rivers flow under my feet? Can you not see (that I am your mighty savior)? (43:51)." Pharaoh and his followers drowned in the Red Sea.

President Morsi is no Pharaoh. Nor is he an Assad or a Mubarak. Morsi is the first genuinely elected president of Egypt, a great nation that leads the Arab region in myriad ways. The remnants of the old regime will do everything to fail Morsi, democracy, and the rule of law. Morsi, as the leader of the Muslim Brotherhood, an Islamic political party, carries a special religious burden to refrain from turning himself into a despot-hero. An anti-hero Egypt will also prevent despotism and strengthen democracy.

P.S. President Morsi was deposed and is now facing murder charges. Egypt has returned to generals and military rule.

2. MOB DEMOCRACY

Mob democracy is a violent form of direct democracy, periodically activated in Pakistan to confuse, frighten, and undermine representative governments established under the Pakistan Constitution.

These days, a mob led by a charismatic politician and a cult figure is marching toward the nation's capital, Islamabad, to demand that the Prime Minister resign and the national parliament be dissolved. The Pakistan high courts, including the Supreme Court, have ruled that such demands, no matter how popular, are unconstitutional and may even amount to treason.

As a system, direct democracy is not the same as representative democracy. Under direct democracy, the decisions are made by the people without a parliament or any other intervening institution. Historically, direct democracy has been a viable political method for decision-making in small cities and towns. In modern nations, referendums and initiatives are the procedures of direct democracy used to settle political questions and make constitutional changes with popular support.

Most nations of the world have rejected direct democracy in favor of representative democracy -a form of indirect democracy under which the people elect a parliament (unicameral or bicameral) and authorize the parliament to make laws, set national policies, form governments, and amend the constitution. Pakistan is a layered representative democracy under which each of the four provinces as well as the federation elects a separate parliament by means of popular vote.

Political Emotionalism

By contrast, mob democracy is popular agitation that thrives on turmoil. It arouses the people to paralyze the government through protests, sit-ins, and the so-called long marches. The leaders heading the mob democracy may use passionate rhetoric, pose open or veiled threats to execute the rulers, and may instigate the mob to disobey the parliament, the courts, the police, and other enforcement agencies critical for the maintenance of law and order.

In defending their course of action, the proponents of mob democracy may invoke several modern human rights, including the right to free speech, the right to association, the right to petition, and the right to justice, to argue that the mob pressure is necessary to unseat the members of an "illegitimate" parliament or the "corrupt" heads of government and state. The proponents may also invoke the right to food, shelter, and other social and economic rights to demand that the system be changed and a new constitution be established.

In Pakistan, where the masses are poor and the basic amenities of life are unavailable, mob mutineers know that they can easily excite the masses by painting the rulers as greedy accumulators of wealth for personal gain. The allegations of rigging the elections are also popular excuses to challenge the government.

In hot summer months made worse due to shortage of

electricity, the passions can run high and a credible case can be made that the government is incompetent and doing little to remedy the problems the people face.

Mob democracy is popular in Pakistan because the politicians of all parties are steeply engrossed in inter-personal power politics. They see gaining power as a game and not a responsibility to solve problems.

Remnants of Moghul Empire

Like the contentious princes of the Moghul Empire, Pakistani politicians spend most of their time and resources in hatching conspiracies to keep or snatch away the throne. Few of them believe that great service to the nation can be rendered by sitting in the opposition and doing the nitty-gritty legislative work.

Gaining executive power is the most valued dream of most Pakistani politicians. Even the provincial executive power does not satisfy their love of personal glory and ambition.

The people of Pakistan need to understand that mob democracy is the worst form of government, worse than the military rule. Mob democracy disrupts normal life, undermines the rule of law, discourages foreign investments, and devalues the national currency. In the fold of mob democracy, the people who suffer the most are ordinary workers and families with limited resources.

The Pakistani media have a special obligation to teach the nation that mob democracy undermines representative democracy, which is neither perfect nor efficient. In every country, representative democracy favors persons with money and networks. It benefits influential families. Yet in an imperfect world, representative democracy delivers more social and economic freedom than any other form of government.

In the final analysis, Pakistan must conclude that the constitutional continuity of democracy is better than rosy revolutions. Short-time problems with political institutions do not justify tearing down a constitutional system. The system may be fine-tuned without rejecting its core structures. Mob democracy is the most dangerous form of politics. It might suit the temper of megalomaniacs and irresponsible demagogues but it weakens the foundation of a responsible political system.

3. POLITICAL EXCLUSION

Iran's Guardian Council, the supreme constitutional body designed to safeguard the rule of Islam, has disqualified thousands of applicants from contesting the February 20 parliamentary election. The election laws allow the Council to disqualify applicants who are found not respecting Islam.

Based on this screening standard, pre-election disqualifications have particularly hit hard among others, the members of the Islamic Iran Participation Front, a reformist political party. Among the disqualified are 80 sitting members of the parliament, including President Khatami's younger brother who heads the Front and accuses the unelected Guardian Council of abusing the rule of law.

Part of the crisis stems from power politics. Political cleansing in the name of Islam is a conservative device to win the elections through disqualification rather than political competition. After losing seats to reformers in the previous election, the religious right, headed by the Guardian Council, is resolved to prevent reformers from reclaiming the parliament. Cleansing would remain incomplete, the Council has concluded, unless both the incumbents and new reformers are simultaneously disqualified from the electoral contest.

To achieve its political objective, the Guardian Council is using election laws to disqualify its opponents for not respecting Islam. But what does the charge of not respecting Islam mean? A case-by-case disqualification might be acceptable if an independent court determines on the basis of solid evidence that an applicant has violated what Iran's constitution calls "the essentials of Islam."

Even judicial decisions are sound only if disqualification standards are clear and constitutionally permissible - for the constitution specifically prohibits investigation of one's beliefs. But when the Guardian Council uses elusive standards and unsubstantiated accusations to disqualify its political opponents *en mass*, an outside observer would conclude that the law of disqualification has become a tool of the intolerant.

In the midst of intolerance, the conception of Islamic democracy itself is at stake. Does Islam allow political dissent and diversity of viewpoints? The Iranian reformers, including President Khatami, are committed Muslims. They do not want to abandon Islam as a guiding force, nor do they wish to establish a secular state. They simply assert that an open democracy, under which political parties with diverse viewpoints are free to contest elections, is compatible with Islam.

A democracy with no normative constraints, the Guardian Council fears, would undermine the theocratic foundation of the republic. Committed to protecting Islam from the corrupting influence of unchecked freedoms, the Guardian Council has been overly vigilant in combating reform ideas.

First, intellectuals have been arrested and newspapers closed. And now the political process is being engineered to eliminate reformers from the parliament. The story of the Council's self-righteousness splattered across the pages of world newspapers gives credence to the stereotype that Islamic democracy is inherently intolerant.

So what can be done? Any radical proposal to dismantle the Guardian Council is unlikely to win popular support. Even the reformers understand that the Iranians are not ready for any big restructuring, let alone for a counter-revolution that would disempower the clerics for good and establish a western-style liberal democracy.

It appears to most observers that Iran will remain an Islamic state in the foreseeable future, unless the Guardian Council through its unreasonable hold on power completely de-democratizes the political process.

To save Islamic democracy from subversion via extremism, the Council must be shepherded away from politics and confined to its constitutionally mandated juristic obligation. The Council can be a valuable juristic institution in overseeing the conformity of parliamentary legislation with the Quran and the Sunnah.

Many Muslim countries, including Afghanistan, are embracing the idea of a juristic council. As a juristic body, however, the Council must not interfere in the ins and outs of political parties and electoral competition. Even in its juristic role, the Council must be pragmatic and open to modernity. It must respect legislative choices of a popularly elected Islamic parliament. For otherwise the Guardian Council would block, as it has in the past three years, much of the legislation passed by what it perceives to be "reformers."

Iran's Supreme Leader must discharge its constitutional obligation in changing the Council's orientation from a political guild to a juristic body. Ayatollah Ali Khameini is a progressive leader who believes in science and development. He has already demanded that the disqualification crisis be settled in accordance with the rule of law, a demand that the reformers have also made.

But the rule of law requires that decision-makers

should not have a blatant political stake in the outcome. As currently oriented, the Guardian Council identifies itself with the conservatives and refuses to acknowledge that Iran cannot develop as a progressive Islamic state unless political competition is free and elected officials are not arbitrarily disbarred from the parliament. De-politicization of the Guardian Council is a gradual process, but it can begin by allowing the reformers to freely contest the February parliamentary election.

4. ANARCHY

Pakistan is a nation full of mutineers who know little about governance, economic development, or international affairs. (I myself was a naïve revolutionary in my early 20s but came to the United States and thankfully lost the fervor after writing a doctoral dissertation on revolutions.) In hot summer months, when the people are suffering from the punishing shortage of water, gas, and electricity, the dapper mutineers of Pakistan, living in comfy homes fortified with maids and servants, yell and roar to change everything bad in the country -- corruption, family favoritism, religious intolerance, honor killings, police brutality, economic injustice, U.S. drone attacks, airport shootings, and scores of other social, political, and economic ills that beleaguer the nation. The problems they identify are real. The solutions they offer are perilous.

The Pakistani mutineers are amazingly diverse. They come in military uniforms, religious costumes, playboy outfits, and even plain clothes. Some mutineers have acquired foreign citizenship, some deliver live speeches from abroad, and some have returned home after frittering joyful youth in Western countries. Most mutineers are home-grown radicals who see little virtue in democratic evolution. Some hold the reins of power but do not believe in the rule of law. Some rebels are driven by dreams of personal glory but the most mesmerizing kind believes that God has chosen them to protect Pakistan. Among the most mesmerizing rebels are Chief Minister Shahbaz Sharif, Altaf Hussain (U.K. citizen), Imran Khan, and Tahir-ul- Qadri (Canadian citizen). General Pervez Musharraf, a world-class mutineer, who overthrew a democratically elected government to grab power, attacked India in Kargil, killed hundreds of seminarians to curb terrorism, and detained the Supreme Court Justices to pursue stardom, is facing treason charges.

Logic of Mutinies

Pakistan is a wonderful laboratory for the world to study the cobweb of anarchy for here the logic of mutinies is unassailable and almost all mutineers have valid points. For example, most politicians are dishonest, uneducated, and spend most of their energies in interpersonal quarrels. Very few develop even elementary knowledge of statecraft. Seeing blatant incompetence of the politicians, the military generals find reasons for mutiny. However, the military generals see the use of force (*dunda* as they say in local languages) as the solution to most problems. Each military general who unlawfully assumed power in Pakistan either dismembered Pakistan or sowed the seeds of dismemberment. Politicians, therefore, find reasons for mutiny against the generals. A persistent tension between the generals and politicians has weakened the primacy of the constitution. A country without stable and reliable rules of succession from one government to the next cannot deliver prosperity to the people.

Pakistani politicians themselves weaken the very constitution under which they are elected or establish federal and provincial governments. Soon after a government assumes power, opposition parties begin to conspire to shorten its constitutional tenure of five years. Mass rallies are staged to disrupt normal life. Public property is destroyed. Open gun battles between the police and protesters break out and are shown on live television. Those who have lost the elections rarely concede with open hearts. The system is so thoroughly corrupt that the charges of vote fraud are always credible. If political parties respect each other's mandate, they are accused of collusion and "match-fixing."

But opposition parties are not the sole mutineers. Even the ruling party begins to misbehave soon after assuming power. Close family members are granted lucrative jobs, political offices, and government contracts. The rule of law is compromised to promote favoritism and punish those who criticize government policies. There can be no light of law when every heart is lost in darkness. No social order is possible when the leaders in power are anarchists and mutineers.

Boring Democracy

Pakistan needs boring democracy, not mesmerizing mutinies (boring means to make a hole in a solid substance with persistent rotation). A nation facing existential problems needs silence, not agitation; patience, not protest; cool-headed hard work, not emotional eruptions. A boring democracy has no use for rebels; it relies on experts and professionals to solve problems. For example, it takes time to build reliable water, gas, and electricity networks. Dependable utilities require technical knowhow, resources, long-term investments, and a transparent accounting system under which services are billed and bills are paid. A boring democracy executes well-planned projects and distrusts orators who promise to fix chronic shortages in a year or so.

Likewise, a boring democracy shuns mass rallies, destruction of public properties, and a politics of ultimatums and deadlines for meeting political demands. Most importantly, a boring democracy shuns fiery rhetoric. It encourages the slow grinding of the rule of law and does not throw away the system if some outcomes are disappointing. It stays the course when the course is rough. A boring democracy urges politicians to use measured and cautious language, and deliver more than they promise. In a boring democracy, elected officials spend most of their time studying problems and developing skills to find creative and durable solutions. They do not waste time on TV talk shows, engaging in fruitless and mutually defamatory accusations. Democracy prospers when the politicians, even if truly boring, are highly competent managers (as some are in Norway and Sweden, the most prosperous and democratic nations on the planet). Pakistan needs to develop a culture of anti-heroism and the people need to be highly skeptical of charismatic mutineers. Those who bring the most benefit for the nation are frequently quiet and self-effacing persons.

5. FACTIONALISM

Bangladesh, the eighth most populated country in the world, is seething with political factionalism and constitutional confusions. Let me first note, however, that, despite ceaseless political turmoil, Bangladesh has secured significant economic growth since its independence in 1971 from Pakistan. The people of Bangladesh are entrepreneurial by temperament. They thrive as merchants, traders, and retailers. Bangladeshi immigrants control the Indian food business in the United Kingdom. Be not surprised to find a Bangladeshi owner behind almost every "Indian restaurant" in London.

With copious initiative, Bangladeshis are taking over the Indian food and other retail businesses in New York City. In Kansas, a Bangladeshi immigrant has opened the first Malaysian fast food restaurant with exclusive rights to expand the franchise throughout the United States. Muhammad Yunus, who won the Nobel Peace Prize in 2006 for pioneering microloans to alleviate poverty, is the luminary of a culture that strives hard to wade through immense difficulty with patience and cunning. Goldman

Sachs predicts that Bangladesh carries the potential of becoming one of the top economies in the 21st century. This economic potential will remain untapped unless Bangladesh overcomes toxic factionalism and constitutional confusions.

Toxic Factionalism

Unfortunately, Bangladesh continues to generate toxic factionalism. The nation is divided into numerous large and small political factions untutored in the science of politics. Emotions run high and irrationality rules decisions. Some factions are prepared to kill each other. Bangladesh typifies a nation where the ruling party, in order to remain in power, spends most state resources in suppressing opposition parties. Old politicians continue to nurse old wounds. Some are unforgiving. The feud between Prime Minister Sheikh Hasina and Former Prime Minister Khaleda Zia is a battle between secularism and Islam. The execution of Abdul Quader Molla for war crimes, even if defensible under the law, has widened the gulf between secular and Islamic political forces. The Bangladesh Supreme Court has turned into a highly secular institution. It found an excellent opportunity to demonstrate its commitment to secularism by converting Molla's life imprisonment into a death sentence. The execution of a prime Muslim leader has strengthened the resolve of local militants to fight what they perceive to be the Hindu-dominated secularism. This development cannot benefit Muslims or Hindus.

Part of toxic factionalism stems from a political culture that promotes family connections and cronyism. Main political parties are hereditary and orbit around well-known political names, Sheikh Mujib (assassinated, 1975), Ziaur Rahman (assassinated, 1981), and Hussain Ershad (recently threatened to kill himself). Minor parties boost political toxicity but remain ineffective in winning parliamentary seats. Democracy cannot deliver peace and prosperity if the people have little option but to elect the same few political leaders in every election. The people of Bangladesh wish that main political parties restrain political meanness. They also demand a political culture that inspires young educated men and women to join political parties and rise through the ranks to top leadership.

Constitutional Confusions

Part of political turmoil stems from Bangladesh's constitutional confusions. A prototypical national constitution serves at least two important goals. First, it articulates the nation's supreme values. Second, it lays down a political procedure by which state power can be peacefully transferred from one government to the next. Unfortunately, the Bangladesh constitution, after the 15th amendment made in 2011, has become a hotchpotch of contradictions and confusions.

Now, the Bangladesh constitution espouses incompatible supreme values, Islam and secularism. The Constitution opens with an Arabic prayer, *BISMILLAH-AR-RAHMAN-AR-RAHIM*, found at the beginning of every chapter (except one) of the Qur'an. The prayer is translated in English: "In the name of Allah, the Beneficent, the Merciful." The 15th amendment inserts an additional translation of the same Arabic prayer: "In the name of the Creator, the Merciful." In replacing the word Allah with creator, the 15th amendment appeases non-Muslims, particularly Hindus (nearly 10 percent of the population). Article 2A of the constitution declares Islam to be the state religion. However, the 15th amendment expands Article 2A to "ensure equal status" to Hinduism and other religions. If the state is obligated to ensure equal status to other religions, it is unclear why the 15th amendment retained Islam as the state religion.

Secularism versus Islam

While the word Islam appears only once in the

constitution, the word secularism appears four times in various constitutional provisions. The preamble to the constitution declares secularism, not Islam, as the high ideal. The 15th amendment modifies Articles 8 and 12 to reinforce secularism. The amended Article 8 declares secularism, not Islam, to be the fundamental principle of state policy. The amended Article 12 prohibits "the abuse of religion for political purposes." In August 2013, the Bangladesh Supreme Court banned the country's largest Islamic party, Jammat-e-Islami, contending that the party's charter conflicts with secular provisions of the constitution. As noted above, the Supreme Court ordered that the leader of Jammat-e-Islami be executed for war crimes. Bangladesh is heading toward political chaos much like what occurred in Algeria and Tunisia, where religious parties were also banned bringing years of political instability and Islamic militancy.

The 15th amendment also deleted the constitutional provisions providing for a caretaker government during general elections. The opposition parties are refusing to participate in the 2014 general elections under the incumbent government. If parties are unable to find a solution to political stalemate, the opposition parties may resort to civil disobedience and deadly protests. The incumbent government may use political unrest as a pretext to postpone elections further deepening political chaos. If protests turn bloody and become unmanageable, a military takeover cannot be ruled out. On the brighter side, an intervening military government, with or without the consent of political parties, might serve as the inevitable caretaker government to hold the 2014 general elections.

6. NEPOTISM

Pakistan has transmuted the customary concept of nepotism into a popular and profitable business. Some experts portray customary nepotism as a biological compulsion. We are hard-wired as a species to take care of our off-springs, siblings, even nieces and nephews. The word nepotism is derived from the Italian word nepote, which means nephew; and, historically, nepotism refers to past practices of the Roman Catholic Popes, who would grant special favors to nephews and other relatives. Currently, however, influential and powerful persons are accused of nepotism when they confer substantial benefits on undeserving family members. Nepotism, favoritism, and cronyism are deeply imbedded in almost all nations. In Pakistan, however, nepotism thrives as a business for profitable networking and money laundering. Morally upright individuals who challenge the nepotism business face retaliation; they are scandalized and discredited.

Sifarish
Sifarish, another name for profitable networking, is the

core element of the nepotism business. Influential and powerful families employ nepotism to gain and retain political and economic power. Others use sifarish to procure plum jobs for their sons and daughters. At the premium levels of nepotism, sifarish safeguards family entitlements. Upon Prime Minister Benazir Bhutto's assassination, her teenager-son assumed the chairmanship of the Pakistan People's Party, the nation's largest political party, and her husband, a man known for corruption, was installed as the nation's president. Hina Khar, the daughter of an influential family, with little education or experience in international affairs, frequently flashing style more than substance in diplomatic conferences, became the youngest person ever to head the nation's foreign ministry. In the nepotism business, sifarish rather than individual competence secures premium political jobs.

Sifarish is not the exclusive prerogative of prominent families. Sifarish has trickled down in deep recesses of the society. Pakistan is a nation where nothing moves without sifarish. State bureaucrats, police officers, even minor clerks, all employ sifarish to collect illegal advantages for themselves and family members. A state bureaucrat uses sifarish to obtain government funds to send his son abroad for higher education. A police officer networks with a local businessman to get a job for his unemployed nephew. A clerk, say working in the revenue department, will liaise with his superiors to reduce someone's tax liability. The clerk will use this illegal favor to obtain money, free movie tickets, free dinner for the family, or whatever the taxpayer can afford. From top to bottom, illegal quid pro quos are traded for a legion of benefits.

Money Laundering

In addition to sifarish, money laundering is integral to the nepotism business. The relatives of influential and powerful individuals exploit their networking contacts to sponsor illegal transactions for a hefty fee, called commission. For example, the Pakistani prime minister's son used his contacts to subvert laws of the International Narcotics Control Board, an international agency that monitors international drug control conventions. He assisted local pharmaceutical companies in obtaining illegal licenses from the Pakistani government to import a chemical known as "Ephedrine" in quantities exceeding the limit set by the International Narcotics Control Board. Such facilitation is of course done for a fee. Islamabad high officials working under the prime minister have prevented enforcement agencies from conducting a proper investigation of the case.

Asif Ali Zardari, the current president of Pakistan, was notorious for making money through commissions while his wife was the prime minster. In 2003, a Swiss magistrate found him guilty of money laundering and ordered that he return $11 million to the Pakistani government.

Just like sifarish, money laundering has permeated the entire society. Big and small operatives network with state bureaucrats, police, airport authorities, and customs and immigration officials to sponsor illegal transactions. They charge a fee if you need to subvert bureaucratic administrative rules or police procedures, solve passport problems or visa complications, or evade customs duties. Every law can be broken for a fee. Roaming in the vicinity of judicial courts, persons are available for a fee to appear as false witnesses in civil and criminal cases. Local lawyers serve as intermediaries between judges and litigants for obtaining favorable judgments for significant "attorney's fees."

Scandalization

Stakeholders gear into retaliatory action if a morally-upright person challenges the nepotism business. Whistle-blowers are punished as traitors. Politicians, journalists, bureaucrats, lawyers, judges, and enforcement officials all are under systemic pressure to cooperate with each other

24

in protecting the nepotism empire. Anyone can profit by serving the nepotism empire and protecting its secrets. The challenger is scandalized and threatened with severe consequences.

Efforts are under way to malign the nation's chief justice who has been a vociferous opponent of nepotism. Using the constitutional suo moto action, the Pakistan Supreme Court has unmasked numerous nepotism networks and associated illegal transactions involving the president, prime minister, bureaucrats, and business barons. This judicial jolting has generated unprecedented resentment. The vested interests are cooking conspiracies to scandalize the chief justice.

The latest scandal incriminates the chief justice's son for receiving millions of dollars from a rich realtor as a quid pro quo for judicial relief that the son promised in dozens of cases pending against the realtor in the Supreme Court. The realtor laid out the allegations in a dramatic press conference, painting the chief justice as a morally dubious person. Opponents of the chief justice, including journalists, politicians, bureaucrats, and lawyers, began to demand that the chief justice resign as he has lost the moral authority to head the Supreme Court.

In a strange twist of events, however, the realtor is caught red-handed conspiring with the media to malign the chief justice. In a talk show on Dunya TV, the realtor makes forceful allegations against the chief justice. During commercial breaks, however, when the cameras are off, the realtor is seen schmoozing and planting the interview with the talk show hosts, producers, and other operatives -- an event secretly filmed and later released on YouTube. The film bares the realtor as a man of consummate manipulation. The film also shows the realtor receiving a phone call from the Prime Minister's son during a commercial break. Mouths drop when the realtor casually boasts that he chats with President Zardari on a regular basis. The film persuades the audience that the realtor is a conspiratorial man in cahoots with the government. The scandal fails but the point is made that the defenders of nepotism will do anything to preserve their empire.

Conclusion

Pakistan, a large Muslim nation, is drifting toward moral anarchy and lawlessness. The joint venture to smear the chief justice exposes the vindictive cynicism of ruling elites. Amidst widespread nepotism, the ordinary citizens face a thoroughly dishonest system where laws are subverted even by the guardians of law. The survival of the chief justice and the sustainability of an independent Supreme Court constitute the last big hope for the people of Pakistan. Otherwise, the burgeoning business of nepotism will completely devour the rule of law.

7. BULLY POLITICS

Pakistan's bully politics breeds political operators who use verbal insults and threats of physical violence to intimidate opponents. For a legion of cultural reasons, Pakistan encourages, protects, and even romanticizes bully politics. Educated, calm, and judicious politicians, with credible knowledge of statecraft, rarely rise to the top leadership of political parties.

Woven around a few wealthy families -- with a history of mistreating servants, employees, farmers, and workers -- most political parties nurture the art of bully politics. Even middle-class politicians figure out pretty early that the way to get popularity and rise to the top of political stepladder is to deliver speeches replete with caustic accusations, foul language, and overt threats to the person and household of political opponents. In some cases, political leaders deliver direct threats to police officers and might even incite their followers to gang up and browbeat policemen.

Like bullies in gang warfare, political bullies have little respect for the rule of law and law enforcement agencies. They view politeness and calm demeanor as points of personal weakness.

Pakistan's bully politics has become most apparent in the recent Islamabad sit-ins in which Oxford-educated Imran Khan and Islamic scholar Tahir ul Qadri have issued threats of violence, engaged in verbal abuse, and incited their followers to attack the national parliament. They are protesting against systemic injustice, poll rigging, and demanding that the Prime Minster resign. Both Khan and Qadri have been raised in Punjab, the most populated province of Pakistan.

Punjabi Culture

Bully politics is the invention of Punjabi culture, even though it is now practiced throughout Pakistan. The Punjabi culture, one of the oldest cultures of the world, is layered with sweetness, joviality, generosity, and light-heartedness. Punjab has produced great mystics, poets, singers, generals, and religious leaders.

Yet, Punjab has a dark side most conducive to bully politics. Punjabis have perfected the science of foul language (گالیاں) and threats of fighting words (دھمکی). Ordinary heated conversations among friends are incomplete without the consumption of foul language, sometimes to adorn the argument. Popular Punjabi jokes reinforce the point that no show of antagonism can be accomplished without hurling filthy curses.

Just like foul language, threats are routinely given to intimidate opponents, neighbors, classmates, shopkeepers, even lawyers and judges. Known as turri (تری) and burruk (برک) in the Punjabi language, these are fighting words employed to extract benefit or cause behavior modification.

Unfortunately, Imran Khan uses both foul language and fighting words in his political speeches. Though Khan has lived in England for many years and was married to a sophisticated English lady, there is little trace of English respectability left in his political conduct. Khan behaves more like a Punjabi villain in an action movie (Maula Jat) rather than an Oxford don. Qadri, a law professor and Sufi, is more restrained in the use of foul language but his fighting words are fiercer than those of Khan. In speeches, Qadri regularly delivers threats to hang the Prime Minister and the Chief Minister of Punjab.

Khan and Qadri are by no means the only politicians who engage in bully politics. Punjab Chief Minister Shahbaz Sharif is on record for using fighting words against President Asif Zardari. Several politicians from Punjab, and some from other provinces, continue to engage in bully politics, frequently openly fighting in popular talk shows. Some talk show hosts take delight in exposing bully politics.

Crude Analysis

In addition to cultural undercurrents, bully politics flourishes the most in countries such as Pakistan where the people are poor and illiterate. Bully politics presumes that the people have little capacity to understand the complex dynamics of economy, sociology, and foreign affairs. Accordingly, politicians resort to crude analysis, articulating national issues in rudimentary concepts such as theft, murder, and injustice, accusing the government of stealing state resources, casting security forces as heartless killers, and painting the prevailing system as the source of all social and economic adversity.

Shunning rational discourse, bully politics speaks the language of emotions and reduces politics to inter-personal rivalries. Leaders are not interested in any serious policy analysis. Some might not even spend any time in learning about the problems that face the nation.

Promoting Civility

As I have been suggesting in prior writings on Pakistan, the free and vibrant electronic media of Pakistan can play a decisive role in transforming bully politics. The media talk show hosts must refrain from staging political cockfights. The hosts themselves must prepare for serious policy analysis and invite politicians and experts who have the requisite knowledge to discuss serious matters facing the nation. They must have zero tolerance for bully politics.

Furthermore, major political parties should seriously consider the dangers of bully politics and develop a national code of political conduct. Each political party may launch its own training programs for coaching leaders and political workers in the art of effective communication with the people.

The national parliament and provincial legislatures are natural places where a political culture based on policy analysis and mutual respect can be cultivated.

8. COLLABORATIVE DEMOCRACY

Neoteric political theories, just like novel laws, can emerge from the concurrence of seemingly irreconcilable facts. Pakistan's collaborative democracy -- a form of government under which the leading political parties engage in dualistic politics of simultaneously governing and sitting in opposition -- has surfaced as a consequence of fortuitous election results. In the 2008 general elections, no political party obtained an absolute majority in the national parliament. The Pakistan People's Party (PPP), which won the most seats in the national parliament, has allied with other parties to form a multiparty national government. The Pakistan Muslim League (N), the second largest party in the national parliament, after a short period of alliance with the PPP, opted out of the national government and it now serves as the leading opposition party. The 2008 elections yielded even more complex results in the four provinces of Pakistan. The PML (N) won a clear majority in the provincial assembly of Punjab, the largest province of Pakistan, and has formed the provincial government. The PPP, the second largest party

31

in the Punjab assembly, is serving as the leading opposition party. The PPP and PML (N), the two leading political parties, are thus simultaneously serving as ruling and opposition parties. This dualistic politics has laid the foundation of what might be called collaborative democracy.

Elements of Collaborative Democracy

A study of Pakistan's political system demonstrates that five elements are needed to institute collaborative democracy. First, a nation must be a federated state and not a unitary state to practice collaborative democracy. However, most nations in the world are unitary states and cannot practice collaborative democracy. Second, the parliamentary form of government, rather than the presidential form of government, is more conducive to collaborative democracy. Third, the democratic system must allow multiple political parties to contest general elections. A single-party state, such as China and North Korea, cannot establish collaborative democracy. Fourth, the leading party should form a multiparty federal government but sit in opposition in one or more provincial assemblies. If a single party sweeps the elections and makes no party alliances to form federal and provincial governments, collaborative democracy cannot be instituted. Fifth, and the most important, the leading political parties should engage in dualistic politics as they govern and sit in opposition at the same time.

The third and the fourth attributes of collaborative democracy listed above are self-evident and need no more elaboration. Other attributes do. Collaborative democracy can be cultivated in federated states, such as India and Pakistan; but, it cannot grow in unitary states, such as Turkey, where a single party may win elections and form the national government. If multiple parties are allowed in a unitary state, such as Israel, a single party may not win a governing majority in the national parliament. In such cases, the leading party may unite with other parties to form a coalition government. A coalition government in a unitary state, however, does not institute collaborative democracy because a leading opposition party may be completely excluded from the government. And if all leading political parties join the coalition government, the system lacks vigorous opposition, the sine quo non for universal democracy. In a federated state, however, collaborative democracy is cultivable since a leading opposition party excluded from the federal government may very well be the ruling party in one or more provinces. As noted above, the PML (N) is the leading opposition party in the federal parliament but it has formed its own government in the province of Punjab.

Furthermore, collaborative democracy may not develop even in federated states that adopt the presidential form of government, such as the United States. In a presidential form of government, an elected president forms the federal government whereas elected governors form provincial (state) governments. The concept of a coalition government is foreign to the presidential form of government. In the United States, a Democratic president may or may not collaborate with a Republican Congress or Republican governors for solving federal and state problems. Frequent gridlocks between the Executive and Congress demonstrate the absence of collaboration. The presidential veto may undermine even a bipartisan majority in the Congress. By contrast, collaboration is indispensable if no single party commands a governing majority in the parliamentary form of government. In Pakistan, the PPP does not have an absolute majority in the national parliament to form its own government. Therefore, the PPP must collaborate with other parties to form the federal government. Furthermore, even if a leading party enjoys an absolute majority in the parliament it may nonetheless form a multiparty government to expand political collaboration. This collaborative flexibility is unavailable in a presidential form of government restricted to a two-party political establishment.

Benefits of Dualistic Politics

Dualistic politics occur when a leading party sitting in opposition is also a governing party, and vice versa. In Pakistan, the PPP and the PML (N), the two leading political parties, engage in dualistic politics of governing and sitting in opposition at the same time. As noted above, the PPP governs the center and is the leading opposition party in the Punjab assembly. The PML (N) governs the province of Punjab and sits in opposition in the national parliament. The PML (N) critiques the PPP policies at the national level whereas the PPP critiques the PML (N) policies at the provincial level. The political alliances in the other three provinces of Pakistan are much more complex and beyond the scope of this analysis; however, these alliances are consistent with collaborative democracy.

Dualistic politics is qualitatively different from conventional politics. In conventional politics, the opposition party is determined to finding flaws in the government and may resort to honest, radical, and even irresponsible criticisms. In dualistic politics, the opposition party is restrained and pragmatic in its criticisms because it itself as a governing party is subject to similar criticisms. For example, the PML (N) reproaches the PPP for not solving the electricity shortage crisis. However, the PPP can similarly reproach the PML (N) for not solving the electricity crisis in the province of Punjab. Surely, dualistic politics can spawn what Imran Khan, the Chief of the Pakistan Tehrik Insaf, calls *nura kushti*, that is, fake fights between the PPP and PML (N). As governing parties, however, the PPP and PML (N) must engage in collaborative democracy to solve problems. They should not undermine each other's government. If they refuse to cooperate, the problems will multiply and both parties will lose seats in the next general elections.

Dualistic politics conducted in a responsible manner is highly valuable in preserving the constitutional system. In Pakistan, conventional politics has been destructive, bordering inanity, which led to military interventions. The leading opposition party with no stake in any government, federal or provincial, has colluded with the military to overthrow the ruling party. Under dualistic politics, the leading opposition party, such as the PML (N), has no incentive in conniving with the military because if the military comes the PML (N) itself will lose power in the province of Punjab. The PPP and PML (N) have a collaborative stake in preserving the constitutional system. Thus, dualistic politics provides a systemic safeguard against foolish conspiracies to unlawfully undermine the ruling party.

Conclusion

The leading political parties are more likely to engage in collaborative democracy when they govern as well as sit in opposition. Collaborative democracy is further strengthened when parties seriously consider building multiparty coalition governments at federal and provincial levels. Efficacious collaborative democracy, however, cannot succeed without vigorous but pragmatic opposition. Leading political parties should find a way to sit in opposition either at the federal or provincial level, but must refrain from undermining each other's government. This dualistic politics of governing and sitting in opposition at the same time will safeguard the constitutional system from degenerative conspiracies, unlawful collusions, and military interventions.

9. LAWYERS ACTIVISM

A lawyers' mutiny is making history in Pakistan. The sight of a "strong and honest" Chief Justice leading the nation's lawyers to oust a military ruler who seized power by removing a democratically elected government makes a fabulous story. The story is even more engaging because the national Parliament elected by the people is playing dead. And the two popular leaders (former Prime ministers Nawaz Sharif and Benazir Bhutto) who could have led the masses in this urgency live happily in exile.

The Parliament's failure to mediate the crisis has forced lawyers across the nation to stage a mutiny against what they call "the usurper of the ship," President Pervez Musharraf. The lawyers are hoping that Musharraf and his crew will jump ship and float away, perhaps to bountiful America.

Hard Lawyering

A senior Supreme Court advocate in Pakistan tells me that this is the first time in Pakistan's history that lawyers have dropped their conflicting political affiliations and forged an unprecedented professional unity to restore the rule of law. More than 80,000 lawyers are acting in solidarity to challenge arbitrary powers that the President exercises on a regular basis with no constitutional authority. The suspension of the Chief Justice on March 9 was the President's most blatant act to intimidate the judiciary. The edifice of law cannot stand and the state cannot survive, says the senior advocate, when the President wearing the uniform of the Army Chief summons the Chief Justice of Pakistan (CJP) into a military camp, grills the CJP in the presence of others including some generals, and then orders his suspension. This Presidential vaulting, I am told, is too much for the lawyers to let stand.

In his petition to the Supreme Court challenging his suspension, the CJP paints the picture of an arrogant President who humiliated his person and his office - "crimes" tantamount to "the subversion of the Supreme Court." On summoning the CJP on April 9, the petition discloses, the President "fervently persuaded him to resign" and made a good many offers to sweeten the forced resignation. The President was "most upset" when the CJP refused to resign. A chain of punitive events followed. The CJP was first detained and prevented from leaving the office for several hours. Later, the CJP and his family were falsely imprisoned in their house. The telephone lines and television connections were cut off to isolate the CJP from the world. Even the Supreme Court brethren could not visit him. The CJP's cars were fork-lifted from his residential premises. On the order of the Supreme Judicial Council, which met the same day in "unholy haste," the CJP's entire staff was taken into custody, harassed, and interrogated. "What was the purpose," asks the CJP?

These stories have stirred many of Pakistan's lawyers into hard action. The lawyers are protesting in the streets to mobilize a popular uprising against the President. They are making it difficult for the Parliament to grant another five years term to the President. They are petitioning the Supreme Court to force the President to leave even earlier.

Soft Dictatorship

Despite an engulfing wave of discontent in the legal profession, a few lawyers do support the President and argue that Musharraf is no tyrant. As a former commando, they say, Musharraf can handle tough assignments. As the President, he is a soft dictator who welcomes (manufactures) testing events to display his power and pragmatism. The Pakistani press, including television, has enjoyed more freedom under his soft authoritarianism than any other time since the creation of Pakistan. The opinion makers and newspaper editors freely trash his policies without hearing a knock at the door in the middle of the night.

Even in the face of killings in Karachi associated with the Chief Justice's failed visit to the city, the President has refused to declare an emergency and suspend fundamental liberties, including the freedoms of speech and association - the rights that empower the lawyers to join hands and protest. The idea of soft dictatorship, perhaps the invention of his legendary legal advisor S.S. Pirzada, has worked well for eight years in lulling the people into political slumber.

While the people and the Parliament are still unsure what to make of the crisis, the lawyers have pooled their resources to fight for a distinct legal objective -suspension annulment.

Suspension Annulment

Pakistan's leading lawyers are seeking the annulment of the CJP's suspension. Soon after the suspension, there existed a small window of time in which the President himself could have undone the worst mistake of his rule. That option is no longer available. Twenty-three

constitutional petitions have been filed with the Supreme
Court, including the one by the CJP, challenging, among
other things, the President's reference under Article 209 of
the Constitution against the CJP, the formation of
Supreme Judicial Council, and sending the CJP on forced
leave and restricting his movements. A larger bench of 13
Justices has been established to rule on these petitions.

The CJP's suspension is indeed the most critical
constitutional issue. Article 209 empowers the President to
form an opinion on information received from any source
that a Supreme Court Judge is incapable of performing the
duties of his office or is guilty of misconduct. The
President may direct the Supreme Judicial Council to
inquire into the matter. Article 209 also provides
procedures for the Supreme Judicial Council to conduct a
hearing and report to the President that a Supreme Court
Judge may be removed from office. Article 211 vests
exclusive jurisdiction in the Supreme Judicial Council to
decide the removal matters and bars "any court" from
calling into question the Council's proceedings, its report
to the President, or its recommendation for the removal of
a Judge. These provisions seem to support the President's
authority to initiate an action against a Supreme Court
Judge. Nonetheless, Article 209 contains enough breathing
space for the Supreme Court to find procedural loopholes
and declare that the President acted without constitutional
authority in suspending the CJP.

If American realism is any guidance to court behavior,
one may safely predict that the Supreme Court will annul
the suspension and restore the CJP to office. This
outcome is most likely because the lawyers of Pakistan will
not be content with anything less. Furthermore, a Supreme
Court Registrar has been murdered. The pro-government
media have launched a campaign to malign some Justices
of the Supreme Court in attempts to undermine the
Court's credibility. In view of these facts, the Supreme
Court is psychologically predisposed to act in self-defense

and will annul the President's reference.

The annulment is most likely to occur, however, because the constitutional petitions are not about the hermeneutics of Article 209 but about a colossal struggle between two primary institutions of Pakistan, the Armed Forces and the Judiciary. Since the creation of Pakistan in 1947, the Supreme Court has sided with the generals who overthrew political governments. The Supreme Court found innovative ways to legitimize military coups, including the one Musharraf staged in 1999. In all these constitutional cases, however, the fight has been between two governments, the military and the political. This time, the fight is between the Judiciary and the Armed Forces. This time, the Judiciary itself is under attack. It is unlikely that the Justices will subordinate themselves to the Generals. In his petition, the CJP prays the Court to annul the President's reference and raises a question that cannot be lightly ignored: "If a contrary view is taken, which judge will then stand up to the executive?"

10. FUSION STATES

In its crusade to democratize the Muslim world, the Bush administration faces the challenges of maximalist democracy—an all-inclusive conception of democracy that generates free and full electoral competition among parties with diverse political platforms. Maximalist democracy loathes diminishing universal suffrage, banning political parties, or restricting political platforms. In the Muslim world, maximalist democracy requires that both Islamic and secular parties be allowed to organize and compete in general elections, and form government upon winning.

At present, a few Muslim nations practice maximalist democracy. Despite military coups, Pakistan and Bangladesh have hung on to maximalist democracy. They allow parties of diverse ideological stripes—Islamic, secular, and communist—to freely compete with each other in the general elections. Iraq's constitution drafted under American occupation has adopted maximalist democracy as well. The constitution permits religious and secular parties to freely participate in the political process. Iraq's maximalist democracy, however, is the inevitable

41

outcome of complex forces that occupation and insurgency have unleashed. After deliberately sensitizing the Sunni and Shia separateness, the US had no option but to allow religious parties to compete for power. The Iraqi example, therefore, furnishes little proof that the US is committed to maximalist democracy.

It appears, though, that the Bush administration, despite its fierce rhetoric against Muslim extremists, is willing to accommodate political Islam. In Afghanistan, the US made no effort to ban religious candidates from running in parliamentary elections. The Taliban were disqualified for their alleged support of terrorism and not for their religious orientation. The Bush administration has not opposed even Hamas, a militant Islamic party designated as a terrorist organization under US laws, in contesting parliamentary elections in Gaza and West Bank. Bush policymakers may have concluded that allowing Islamic parties to participate in electoral competition might in fact moderate political Islam—a goal that the US is determined to pursue.

Notwithstanding these concessions to political Islam, the US does not promote maximalist democracy as a matter of principle. Consider the US attitude toward Turkey and Iran, two Muslim nations that repudiate maximalist democracy from opposite viewpoints.

The Turkish constitution embodies irrevocable secularism. And the Turkish army is opposed to political Islam. Political parties that propose to change the Republic's secular characteristics are banned under the constitution. Turkish democracy is open only to secular parties. In recent years, Islamic parties have made some headway, as evidenced by pro-Islamic Erdogan's rise to power. They must still publicly declare their commitment to constitutional secularism. The US is unlikely to pressure Turkey to change its secular constitution to make room for maximalist democracy, where Islamic parties may contest elections on the basis of their religious, rather than secular, political platforms. Lack of pressure aside, no US administration has criticized Turkey for instituting a secular monopoly.

The US is quick to vilify Iran for repudiating maximalist democracy, but no U.S. administration has criticized Turkey for instituting a secular monopoly.

Ironically, though, the US is quick to vilify Iran for repudiating maximalist democracy. This is because Iran is a democratic theocracy. Its constitution establishes a fusion state under which all civil, penal, financial, economic, administrative, cultural, military, political, and other laws and regulations must be based on Islamic criteria. This principle applies absolutely to every aspect of law. As such, no political party that challenges the fusion of state and Islam is allowed to participate in the electoral process. The Council of Guardians screens candidates for their commitment to the fusion principle. Maximalist democracy requires that Iran change its constitution and allow secular parties to contest elections. Even though the fusion provisions of Iran's constitution are theoretically amendable, the ruling clerics would not allow maximalist democracy to challenge the Republic's theocratic monopoly.

When the Bush administration praises Turkey but condemns Iran, its commitment to maximalist democracy seems arbitrary, even anti-Islamic. In praising Turkey, the Bush administration contends that Turkey has successfully combined Islam and democracy. This admiration of Turkey suggests the U.S. favors secular democracy, which allows the people to freely practice their faith, but refuses to accommodate political Islam. In condemning Iran, US officials leave no doubt that Iran fails to meet the standards of maximalist democracy, even though Iran has successfully held periodic presidential and parliamentary elections. "The regime in Teheran must heed the democratic demands of the Iranian people," says Bush, "or lose its last claim to legitimacy."

From these conflicting reactions to political
monopolies in Turkey and Iran, one might conclude that
the U.S. favors secular democracy but opposes political
Islam. This conclusion, however, does not explain the US
policy in Iraq, Afghanistan, and Palestine, where the US
has allowed political Islam to participate in the democratic
process.

It appears the US prefers that Muslim nations adopt
secular liberal democracy. Pragmatism dictates otherwise.
The Bush administration seems to have accepted political
Islam as a reality. Accordingly, it is prepared to allow
Islamic parties to compete with secular forces, particularly
in nations where political Islam has slim chances of major
victory. This pragmatism, however, does not champion
political Islam. When a Muslim nation excludes Islamic
parties from the political process, the U.S. is unlikely to
vouch for political Islam, although the U.S. may pay lip
service to the human rights of the excluded Muslim
groups. For example, the U.S. may criticize Egypt and
Algeria for mistreating the members of Islamic parties, but
it is unlikely to press for maximalist democracy.

Diverse nations have every right to construct new
conceptions of democracy, which respond to their
religious, economic, and social needs.

In my book, *A Theory of Universal Democracy* (2003), I
have argued that Fukuyama's secular liberal democracy
cannot be the end of human history, simply because we are
not at the end of human intelligence. Diverse nations have
every right to construct new conceptions of democracy,
which respond to their religious, economic, and social
needs. While secular liberal democracy has served many
nations well, it cannot be universalized. No view of
democracy must force Muslim nations to oust their
religious traditions from the parameters of law and state.
Muslims have every right to institute a fusion state that
combines rather than separates law and Islam. Exercising
this right, however, Muslim nations must protect the

fundamental liberties of religious minorities. An Islamic system is most acceptable when it embraces maximalist democracy, allowing secular parties to challenge the official ideology—something that Iran does not permit.

Even One God, Islam's ultimate source of instruction, is generously maximalist. God allows Satan to compete fully and freely in God's universe and challenge His conception of virtue and good life. Muslim nations should institute maximalist democracy for launching a free competition between secular and religious forces. Whether the US will consistently support an all-inclusive democracy is an unsure bet...

11. PROSECUTING GENERALS

Pakistani politicians are faltering in their resolve to prosecute General Pervez Musharraf for high treason. Under Article 6 of the Pakistan constitution, "any person who abrogates or subverts or suspends or holds in abeyance, or attempts or conspires to abrogate or subvert or suspend or hold in abeyance, the Constitution by use of force or show of force or by any other unconstitutional means shall be guilty of high treason." This far-reaching language was drafted to deter military generals from seizing power. In 1999, Musharraf did topple a democratically elected government. However, the treason case for which Musharraf is being prosecuted involves the 2007 subversion of the constitution -- a move directly assaulting the independence of judiciary.

In 2007, Musharraf did not overthrow a civilian government. This time Musharraf staged a coup against the Pakistan Supreme Court. By 2007, under an emerging lawyers' movement to restore democracy, the judiciary had been emboldened to stand up to the military generals. Fearing a non-cooperative Supreme Court, Musharraf

46

found a way to remove the antagonistic judges. Invoking the non-existing powers of the Chief of Army Staff, Musharraf passed a new ordinance, prescribing a fresh Oath of Office for all Judges of the Supreme Court and High Courts. Many Judges refused to comply. Some Judges were not even invited to take the Oath. A few Judges of the Supreme Court, including the Chief Justice of Pakistan, were put under house arrest.

Nowhere does the constitution empower the Chief of Army Staff to demand a fresh Oath of Office from Judges of Superior Courts. This brazen constitutional subversion lies at the core of the high treason case against Musharraf.

Political Wisdom

The political elite of Pakistan are divided over the prosecution of General Musharraf. The party in power favors prosecution. Musharraf's name has been placed on the Exit Control List, which means that he cannot leave the country though he has been granted bail in all outstanding cases. While a listless prosecution is moving at a snail pace, some prominent politicians are speaking against the wisdom of prosecution. They prefer that the prosecution be halted and Musharraf be allowed to leave the country.

The pro-Musharraf forces make several pragmatic arguments. Two arguments carry the most traction. First, they argue that the military establishment opposes the Musharraf prosecution. Therefore, antagonizing the generals does not serve the larger interests of Pakistan, particularly at a time when the military is fighting in North Waziristan. Second, they argue that the government should focus on solving more pressing problems, including poverty and shortage of energy, rather than wasting time and resources on prosecution. The party in power is losing steam in making a strong case for the finality of prosecution, and pro-Musharraf forces seem to be gaining momentum.

Law's Wisdom

It is unclear how Pakistani lawyers and judges feel about letting Musharraf go. Lawyers need to be more vocal in expressing their views. After all, the 2007 constitutional subversion was not against politicians or elections; it was against Judges and the rule of law. Musharraf invoked arbitrary powers to dismiss and detain Judges, not politicians. Lawyers know that a nation without an independent judiciary lacks stability and eventually fails. That is why the independence of judiciary is a core principle of contemporary human civilization regardless of culture, religion, political system, and form of government. When judges are at the mercy of rulers, law is no longer a vital force.

While politics is the name of compromise, law is much more complex. Surely, law allows negotiated solution, mediation, conciliation, and settlement of disputes. Relentless compromising, however, is not the wisdom of law. Law needs to be sturdy in select cases. For example, the perpetrators of torture, rape, and genocide cannot be allowed to settle their crimes. The society has a stake in the prosecution of certain crimes even if the victims are willing to forgive and forget.

The Pakistan constitution rightfully identifies constitutional subversion as high treason. Arbitrary dismissal and detention of the Judges of Superior Courts is unforgivable. The treason case is showing the nation that law can reach the high and the mighty. Any political compromise that weakens the sturdy hand of law and finds a way for Musharraf to escape the charges of constitutional subversion will be a regrettable choice. The Pakistan Supreme Court needs to be vigilant in making certain that the law is not compromised

12. WISE GENERALS

Discarding the historical logic of military coups, the Pakistan Army will this time defend the Constitution and not allow the protest leaders to force resignation of the Prime Minister and dissolution of the National Parliament and Provincial Assemblies.

By letting political forces sort themselves out, the Pakistan Army will emerge as one of the most trusted state institutions, no less revered than the independent judiciary and free press. General Raheel Sharif can restore the dignity of the armed forces that Pervez Musharraf squandered away by pursuing personal glory.

It is no secret that the Generals are most respected when they are not running the country. A civilian government fears the armed forces and respects, though with a tinge of resentment, the Generals' geopolitical views, defense plans, and foreign policy preferences. The Generals have more clout behind the veil of a civilian government.

This is not the time for a military takeover. The Pakistani Generals have no interest in running the federal and provincial governments, given the enormous economic, sectarian, ethnic, and political problems that the nation faces. While fighting the Pakistani Taliban and facing a post-invasion Afghanistan, the Generals do not wish to antagonize a sizable portion of the public, including the press, that opposes military governments.

By staging a military takeover, the Generals will face discomforting uncertainty. The United States and the European Union will likely impose military sanctions. The Generals will be under pressure to tow the U.S. line in Afghanistan as was General Musharraf. The case for the denuclearization of Pakistan, a case in the making, will gather a bit more strength.

Even domestically, the Generals will reap no significant benefit by dismantling the Constitution. They will face a vibrant press and a powerful judiciary. The Generals cannot backwind the freedom of press or judicial independence. Repression is no longer available.

Nor can the Generals count on the protest leaders, Imran Khan and Tahir ul Qadri, for political cover though each has a sizeable following among the people. Surely, the grievances of protest leaders are legitimate. The system needs to be fixed to accommodate their genuine demands that would eventually benefit the nation. Yet, the protest leaders provide little effective sponsorship for the armed forces.

Unfortunately, Imran Khan, a popular icon, comes across as a Quixote fighting non-existent windmills. He lacks the intellectual and temperamental stability to lead a nuclear Muslim nation located in a tough neighborhood. His antagonism to the United States and questionable support for the Taliban muddles his candidacy for the prime job.

Tahir ul Qadri, a religious leader loved by his devotees, is a divisive figure. He cannot unite the nation since many religious groups strongly oppose his views about Islam. To make matters worse, he is surrounded by discarded politicians of the past.

Even if protest leaders invite the Generals to unseat the government, most political parties are united against the imposition of martial law or overthrowing the present government. Any military undermining of the Constitution will unleash forces that the Generals will be unable to contain. It is better for the system to work its way through the difficulty.

The armed forces will be the true winners if the Generals let the politicians sort out the mess. There is no credible evidence that the Generals are planning to shake the boat.

13. FAILED REVOLUTIONS

The peoples' revolution is brewing in Tunisia, Yemen, and Egypt. These nations, unlike the Kingdom of Saudi Arabia, have established state constitutions that promise a democratic form of government and espouse the principle of popular sovereignty. Article 3 of the Tunisia Constitution declares that "The sovereignty belongs to the Tunisian People who exercise it in conformity with the Constitution." Article 4 of the Yemen Constitution declares that "Power rests with the people who are the source of all powers." Article 3 of the Egypt Constitution proclaims that "Sovereignty is for the people alone who are the source of authority." Invoking these constitutional provisions, the people of Tunisia, Yemen, and Egypt have resolved to enforce their democratic rights and liberties.

In blatant violation of national constitutions, President Zain El-Abidine Ben Ali ruled Tunisia for twenty four years (1987-2011), President Ali Abdul Saleh of Yemen has been in power for over twenty years (1990-2011), and President Hosni Mubarak of Egypt has occupied the highest state office for thirty years (1981-2011). The people have finally elected to recall these irremovable Presidents by resorting to street power, the ultimate expression of sovereignty against tyranny.

The reasoning of the peoples' revolution is no other but the one that has inspired other revolutions: "When a long train of abuses and usurpations, pursuing invariably the same object evinces a design to reduce (the people) under absolute despotism, it is (the people's) right, it is their duty, to throw off such government, and to provide new guards for their future security." The peoples of Tunisia, Yemen, and Egypt can no longer tolerate sham democracies.

Sham Democracies

It is commonplace in North Africa and the Middle East to establish irremovable autocracies through the medium of sham democracy. Over the decades, sham periodic elections have been held in Tunisia, Yemen, and Egypt to elect parliaments and presidents. However, the same ruling party returns to power and the same President wins an overwhelming majority of popular vote. The periodic democratic ritual is staged to delude the people and the world that the governments in Tunisia, Yemen, and Egypt are anchored in the will of the people. Nothing is farther from the truth.

In October 2009, Tunisia held sham presidential and parliamentary elections. The Constitutional Democratic Rally, the ruling party that has governed Tunisia since its independence from France in 1956, received nearly 85% of the popular vote. To conceal electoral fraud, the ruling party refused international monitoring of the elections. In Egypt, the National Democratic Party has retained power since its creation in 1978.

In the most recent sham elections held in 2010, the National Democratic Party won 81% of the seats in the national legislature. Opposition parties that could have challenged the ruling party were banned and their leaders arrested. Yemen is essentially a one party state. The next parliamentary elections are scheduled to be held in April, 2011. It remains to be seen whether the Yeminis would allow the General People's Congress, the ruling party, to return to power.

Even sham democracies are tolerable if rulers are competent and just. But sham democracies are doubly unbearable if the people face unremitting economic hardships. Hope is at the lowest ebb when protesters wave baguette as the symbol of revolution. In Tunisia, President Ben Ali and his family exploited state power to amass huge amount of personal wealth. Corruption at the top trickled down to the bottom.

Tunisian protests began the day a farmer set himself on fire when the police, in order to extort money, impounded his vegetable and fruit stand. Yemen, the poorest country in the region, has made little economic progress under President Saleh's incompetent administration. In Egypt, Hosni Mubarak has run the state as a personal fiefdom. The members of the ruling party are blissful and affluent whereas millions of ordinary people live in shanties. Economic hardships are further aggravated when omnipresent security forces resort to cruelty, torture, and inhumane treatment.

United States Support

It is unclear how the United States would react to the peoples' revolution in Tunisia, Yemen, and Egypt. While the Obama administration has expressed lukewarm support for Tunisians after Ben Ali's departure, no real support is offered to the peoples of Yemen and Egypt. If history is any guide, the U.S. would give public lectures on the people's right to peaceful protest but secretly support the suppression of revolts in Yemen and Egypt.

As usual, concrete U.S. interests will trump the peoples' right to institute representative governments. The U.S. would support President Saleh for his commitment to physically eradicate al-Qaeda, which is taking root in Yemen. Likewise, the U.S. would support President Mubarak for his commitment to suppress the Muslim Brotherhood, a religious political party that opposes U.S. policies in the Middle East. The despots have memorized the logic of American self-interest.

By betting on the discredited Presidents of Yemen and Egypt, however, the U.S. will choose the wrong side of the inevitable revolution. The revolution for genuine democracy, even if brutally suppressed, is unlikely to fade away. The people seem determined to enforce the national constitutions that promise free and fair elections, freedom of speech, the right to vote, and the right to remove a ruling party that no longer serves their social and economic needs.

In his 2009 speech in Cairo, President Obama rejected the notion of pawning other nations for securing American interests. He said, "For human history has often been a record of nations and tribes subjugating one another to serve their own interests. Yet in this new age, such attitudes are self-defeating. Given our interdependence, any world order that elevates one nation or group of people over another will inevitably fail." Now is the time for President Obama to support the peoples of Tunisia, Yemen, and Egypt in their sovereign struggle to self-enforce the democratic constitutions that have yet to deliver genuine democracy.

14. MINIMIZING CONFLICTS

The time has arrived to cut a new path for the Indic nations. India and Pakistan should consider a defense pact, safeguarding each other's territorial integrity and political independence. This historic reversal of past enmity will lead the two nations toward a bold new future, one free of mutual attrition and bullying by foreign powers.

"It's not going to work," has been the first response of the people with whom I have shared the idea. Set against this unexamined pessimism, the idea of a defense pact is derived from a simple intuition that enemies can become friends by sharing mutual interests.

Sharing more than six thousand years of history, India and Pakistan will breach no taboo if they unite for defense purposes. One caution, however, is appropriate. It is neither probable, nor is it pragmatic, to stitch together the historic pieces of ancient India into a single nation-state, as some Hindu fundamentalists demand. Nor can India be re-created in the form of a single Hindu or Muslim empire, as it has been done in the past. Any such nationalistic or imperial unification of the subcontinent is a fool's dream.

But a defense pact to pool armed resources, primarily to deter foreign aggression, alien domination, and international short-changing is a need that India and Pakistan cannot, and must not, deny.

Denying such a need would be easy if the defense pact is seen through the Kashmir dispute the root cause of problems between India and Pakistan. One might argue that no meaningful relationship, let alone a defense pact, is possible unless the Kashmir dispute is first resolved. This way of thinking is an error.

By all means, the people of Kashmir deserve the right of self-determination. However, they would not lose such a right to freedom if the subcontinent is made safe from external threats. In fact, the defense pact might convince both India and Pakistan that a peaceful and free Kashmir within the boundaries of mutual defense is an excellent idea and a very good deal for all parties. Thus, the defense pact could change the psychology of separation as well as forced assimilation.

Most importantly, the defense pact will reduce unnecessary expenditure on weapons and armies, as the two nations begin to complement each other's military assets and capabilities. The savings from the defense pact can be devoted to raising the standard of living in the subcontinent.

The economic and social dividends of the defense pact will restore the dignity of the subcontinent in world affairs. A subcontinent united by means of a defense pact will become a formidable force in international organizations, including the United Nations. A militarily united subcontinent may also demand a permanent seat in the Security Council. Even if global benefits do not materialize, regional benefits will most certainly accrue. For example, the developing tension between China and the United States, and a possible future war between the two, will be less harmful to the subcontinent if India and Pakistan are militarily united against any threats, incentives, and pressures to take sides in the Sino-American rivalry.

The idea of a defense pact may disappoint those who will lose leverage over a militarily unified subcontinent. But it should surprise no one.

Already, India and Pakistan have put in place the beginnings of a defense pact through a special agreement signed in 1991. According to this agreement, each year, on New Year's Day, India and Pakistan exchange lists of nuclear facilities. They have been doing this for last 12 years, without cheating, reluctance, or bad faith.

The 1991 special agreement has been designed to prohibit the rivals from attacking each other's power plants and nuclear installations. Interestingly, the facilities listed constitute a secret that nobody else in the world is supposed to know. This mutual trust can be the basis for a more expansive defense relationship between the two countries.

Of course, the defense pact is no panacea for the problems that India and Pakistan face. Nor is it going to automatically remove internal and external threats to the subcontinent. But it might provide some hope to the people of the subcontinent that India and Pakistan will not remain divided and ruled from abroad, like in the bad old days of colonialism. The people of the subcontinent must opt for a smarter future than the one submitted to foreign control.

15. CONVOLUTION

Pakistan continually draws world attention. The Taliban, Osama bin Laden, Malala Yousafzai, the ban on NATO supplies for nearly six months, armed Pakistanis invading Mumbai, the Sufi songs of Nusrat Fatah Ali Khan, the Burka Avenger, Ms. Marvel, these and other stories offer a perplexing picture of Pakistan -- the sixth largest nation in the world and owning a stockpile of nuclear weapons possibly exceeding that of the United Kingdom and France. Pakistan, an ancient land baked with layers of Hinduism, Buddhism, Sikhism, and Islam, is a complex and intriguing nation preparing to play a more assertive geopolitical role in the coming decades.

Composed of distinct peoples who have lived in separate enclaves for centuries, including Punjabis, Pashtuns, Sindhis, and Balochis, Pakistan is striving hard, though unsuccessfully, to forge a new national identity. However, inter-ethnic dissensions linger. Few Punjabis would ever marry Sindhis, Pashtuns, or Balochis, and vice versa. Each ethnic group is proud of its history and traditions. The Pashtuns celebrate themselves as indomitable warriors. The Balochis find roots with Iranians and Arabs. The Sindhis are the first Muslims in the subcontinent. The Punjabis, constituting the majority of the population, profess intellectual superiority over others and dominate federal bureaucracy, politics, and the armed forces.

Partly because of ethnic diversity and partly because of a robust oral culture, Pakistanis have a keen sense of regional geopolitics. Much like Iranians, though not as much, Pakistanis are a poetic people. Most Pakistanis are multilingual, speaking at least two languages. The educated Pakistanis may know five to six languages, including Arabic, Persian, and English. Urdu, the national language, is itself a composite language that draws its vocabulary from at least fifteen other languages. Pakistanis are enigmatic in social attitudes, scientific in the day and superstitious at night, chivalrous but erratic in combat, charitable even when impoverished, continuously oscillating between haughty self-confidence and panic-stricken inferiority complex. Pakistanis claim to be the heirs to a thousand years of Muslim rule in India. Yet in folk stories and TV shows, Pakistanis ridicule the memories of Moghul Emperors. They adore cricket and yet make the cruelest jokes about the British Raj.

Pakistanis are nervous neighbors. They have no desire whatsoever to merge with India or live under the same flag with Hindus and Sikhs. The Pakistani soul is incorrigibly puritan and prejudiced. Pakistanis do not even miss losing Bangladesh, once East Pakistan, on the dubious theory that the Bangladeshis did not deserve to be Pakistanis. The China-Pakistan friendship, claimed as "taller than the mountains and deeper than the oceans," bears an eerie halo of reality but it is frequently deployed to cause commotion in the minds of American policymakers whenever Pakistan is cornered or bullied. Because of many material benefits received from the Gulf States, Pakistanis ingratiate Saudi Arabia and the United Arab Emirates as benefactors. Culturally, though, Pakistanis have little amity for the Middle East. Because of the Shia theocracy in Iran, Pakistanis hesitate from forming closer ties with Iran. In their gilded dreams, Pakistanis wish to colonize Afghanistan, one way or the other, to expand their influence over Central Asia. To that end, Pakistanis created the Taliban.

Pakistanis have a schizophrenic relationship with the United States. They admire the U.S. material achievements, its people, its inventions, and its cultural freedoms. They have been receiving U.S. financial assistance ever since Pakistan came into being. During the cold war, Pakistan stood with the United States. For the most part, American generals admire Pakistani generals and defer to their geopolitical judgments.

However, there have been rough spots over military strategies in Afghanistan. When Pakistanis disagree with their American counterparts, Pakistanis play a highly convoluted game that befuddles American policymakers who tend to be linear, forceful, and prosaic. For example, Pakistanis continue to allow drone attacks in tribal areas and sometimes solicit drone attacks for hitting certain targets. The CIA thankfully accommodates Pakistani demands. Yet Pakistani policymakers have launched a vigorous international campaign to argue that drone attacks are unlawful. Most legal experts, the United Nations, geopolitical tacticians, and even ordinary Americans condemn and criticize drone attacks.

Profoundly paranoid, Pakistanis believe that the United States is determined to take away their nuclear bombs. Many Pakistanis fear that after taking the chemical weapons away from Libya and Syria and after imposing draconian sanctions on Iran for its nuclear ambition, the United States and its allies are bound to come after their country too. While fears linger and the chronic electricity shortage aggravates their days and nights, Pakistanis continue to cherish the dreams of defeating India in

Kashmir, the dreams of colonizing Afghanistan, the dreams of defeating the world in Cricket, and the dreams of seeking sovereign equality with the United States.

16. VEILING IN THE WEST

In line with the feminist bumper sticker "Well-behaved women do not make history," Aishah Azmi, a Muslim woman born in Cardiff and raised in Birmingham, is determined to disobey the British male elite and make history. Azmi fully veils her face in the public, including at the school where she taught young girls and boys. No parents or female colleagues at the school objected to her choice of dress. Over the complaint of a British male colleague, however, Azmi was suspended from the job. As the controversy grew, some parents joined the opposition to the veil, complaining that students could not hear Azmi speaking behind the veil. Azmi offered to drop the veil while teaching if no male colleagues were present. The school declined the offer. As a woman of will and determination, Azmi too has refused to give up her identity in public spaces. She is in the process of defending her rights through the British legal system. Though she has lost her case in the first administrative hearing, she intends to appeal to the higher courts.

Politicization of Veil

Instead of allowing the system to freely and fairly process Azmi's legal claim, the British male elite wasted no time in condemning the veil as a profound violation of the British culture. The debate is no more narrow or legal. It is racial and religious.

All over the world, the law permits employers to impose reasonable grooming standards on employees. For example, the police officers may be prohibited from donning hippie hair and the schoolteachers may not be permitted to wear short skirts. Azmi will have a weak legal claim if the school can show a factual linkage between veil and teaching inefficacy. But that is not the point the British male elite, though known for their love of legal formalisms, is making. Their argument goes beyond the grooming standards at workplace. They wish to assimilate immigrant women into a prototypical woman who caters for male sensibilities and makes men feel comfortable.

British Male Attacks

Former Foreign Secretary Jack Straw (who loves to cook puddings in free time) cast the first stone when he requested that Muslim women drop the veil. Straw attempted to intellectualize his request by a louche admission that he watches the facial expressions of women when he engages in conversations with them. The veil prevents him, says Straw, from fully understanding what Muslim women are saying—-not because he cannot hear them but because he cannot see their faces. (I wonder if Straw listens to the radio or ever talks on the phone.)

While Straw flirted with unconvincing logic, Mr. Phil Woolas, a local government minister, came down on the veil with a hard hammer. Mr. Woolas minced no words in issuing a forceful fatwa that the veil provokes "fear and resentment" among the British people. Woolas tried to influence the legal debate as well by openly suggesting that Azmi "can't do her job" wearing a face veil.

While the case was still pending before the tribunal, Prime Minister Tony Blair also entered the furor, smearing the veil as a "mark of separation." Wearing his familiar postiche smile, Blair argued that the veil "makes other people uncomfortable." Fully exploiting the office of the Prime Minister, Blair supported the school's decision in suspending Azmi from the job. Another male from the British ruling elite, higher education minister Bill Rammell, added prejudicial perspective to his colleagues' crusade by reminding the forgetful British public that Imperial College in London had already banned face veils in class.

In this perfervid air of British xenophobia, one important voice arose to protest. Trevor Philipps, the head of the Commission of Racial Equality and a man of African descent, warned that the debate over the veil had "turned ugly" and could spark violence. What is needed, said Mr. Philips, is a gentle and refined discussion. His warning came true within hours when racially charged hoodlums attacked male worshippers at a mosque in Greater Manchester.

Undeterred by these attacks, the British elite continue to trash the cultural identity of a fellow citizen from Cardiff. Meanwhile, history with its inexhaustible ironies offers additional insights into the British resentment against the Islamic veil.

Common Law Coverture

For centuries, the British male elite have served as hysterical vigilantes against assertive women who, like Aishah Azmi, wish to maintain their self-identity in public spaces. In his Commentaries on the Laws of England, William Blackstone defines coverture as follows: "By marriage, the husband and wife are one person in law: that is, the very being or legal existence of the woman is suspended or consolidated into that of the husband: under whose wing, protection and cover, she performs everything." The law of coverture, though wrapped in the romance of a delightful marriage (for man), drew its vicious logic from colonization as the British male elite fictionalized the household in terms of a small colony under the husband's viceroyalty, a colony in which the wife's property came to be vested in husband and in which she was disqualified from entering into separate contracts. These female disabilities were considered necessary to promote the "superior" British culture at home and abroad. Women who refused to get married for fear of losing personal and property rights were regarded as "redundant women."

The common law coverture gradually lost its grip over the British women. The British male elite are now resurrecting coverture to subjugate immigrant women. The new coverture turns the old coverture on its head. The old coverture coerced white women to promote the Victorian vision of separate spheres——homes for women and markets for men. The new coverture compels immigrant women from Asia, Africa, and the Middle East to abandon their unique identities in public spaces. For white women, the old coverture created and enforced the separation of gender spheres; for immigrant women, the coverture imposes the fusion of gender spheres. In each case, some women must lose their identity. In all cases, coverture forces women, white or black, to constantly adjust their identities to make the British men feel comfortable.

Obtuse Logic

There is yet another irony in the veil controversy. In 1991, Fatima Mernissi's book Le Harem Politique (1987) was translated into English with a more descriptive title, *The Veil and the Male Elite*. Analyzing sociological roots of the Islamic veil, Mernissi contends that the Arab male elite of the first few decades of Islam concocted the sacred sources to impose a controlling and oppressive headgear on women. The Prophet was egalitarian, says Mernissii, but his men were not. His men first solicited gender discrimination from the Prophet; and after his death, they fell back into the pre-Islamic days of ignorance and fabricated the Prophet's sayings to perpetuate gender inequality and the veiling of women. True Islam, Mernissi seems to conclude, would let Muslim women choose whether they want to wear the veil.

Few scholars in the Muslim world agree with Mernissi's theological or sociological theses, even though the face veil (*niqab*) is far from a universal value in Muslim countries. Ironically, the British male elite will also hesitate to embrace Mernissi's book. Mernissi is a feminist who wishes to expand the choices women may exercise in public spaces. Mernissi criticizes the "oppressive veil" as a male imposition. She would nonetheless allow women the freedom to wear the veil.

In condemning the veil, however, the British male elite are not making the freedom argument. They are not arguing that woman like Azmi are oppressed and that they must have a choice. In fact, these men spurn the choice argument. They are advocating gender integration for personal convenience. Immigrant women must not wear the veil in public, they say, because the veil is a mark of separation, the veil makes British men feel uncomfortable, and the veil does not allow British Jacks and Joes to watch Muslim women's facial expressions. No self-respecting woman will accept this obtuse logic.

It appears that the British male elite are determined to direct and dictate women according to their personal preferences. They perhaps do not realize that their forced unveiling of Muslim women is no different from their forced domestication of Victorian women.

17. WESTERN ACADEMIC ATTACKS
ON ISLAM

The book titled "*Hagarism: The Making of the Islamic World,*" questions just about everything Muslims believe as historical truths. It challenges the common belief that the Quran was revealed to Prophet Muhammad over a period of 22 years (610-632) in Mecca and Medina. Instead, the book contends that the Quran was composed, possibly in Syria or Iraq, more than fifty years after the Prophet's death, projected back in time, and attributed to the Prophet.

The Quran, according to the book, was fabricated during the reign of Caliph Abdul Malik (685-705) to legitimize an expanding empire. The book also contends that the word Muslim was invented in the 8th century to replace the word Muhajirun (immigrants), which was the original name of the Arab community that conquered Palestine and built the Dome of the Rock.

The book itself prescribes a new name for early Muslims. It calls them Hagarenes, that is, the biological descendants of Abraham by Hagar. This racial naming of early Muslims is employed to distinguish them from Jews, who are the descendants of Abraham by Sarah. Hagarism, the book's title, is a quasi-pejorative, and possibly a racist, label to describe the historical phenomenon of early Muslims.

In the authors' own words, the book is written "by infidels for infidels." Attacks on the Quran's authenticity, the Prophet's integrity, or Islamic history are not new. The Quran itself acknowledges similar attacks the unbelievers made while the Quran was being revealed. For more than a thousand years, Western scholarship has been determined to expose what it considers to be the "fraudulent foundation" of Islam. In this sense, Hagarism is yet another book in the large dump of attack literature.

However, what distinguishes this book is the fact that its authors, Michael Cook and Patricia Crone, no longer subscribe to its critical findings. On April 3, 2006, I had a phone conversation with Michael Cook and we talked about Hagarism. He said to me the following, which he later confirmed by means of an email: "The central thesis of that book was, I now think, mistaken. Over the years, I have gradually come to think that the evidence we had to support the thesis was not sufficient or internally consistent enough."

On April 6, 2006, I interviewed Patricia Crone, as well, to see what she now thinks about the book. She was even more candid in repudiating the central thesis of the book. She agrees with the critics that the book was "a graduate essay." The book was published in 1977 when the authors lived in England. "We were young, and we did not know anything. The book was just a hypothesis, not a conclusive finding," said Crone. "I do not think that the book's thesis is valid."

Many Western scholars, Christians and Jews, have dismissed Hagarism as a "thin argument" rather than "credible research." One historian, however, who appears to admire the book, is Daniel Pipes, who has taught at

Chicago and Harvard universities. Pipes, an embittered Zionist known for his ugly utterings against Islam and Muslims, argues that while Western scholars like Crone and Cook "in the role of termites" are eating away at the magnificent Islamic edifice, Muslims are "acting as though the beams and joints were as strong as ever." Even Pipes, however, describes the book as "wild." Notwithstanding scholarly repudiations, Internet websites continue to rely on the book to malign Islam, assuming that the book's thesis is derived from credible research.

Even online Wikipedia features the book, citing a large quotation from Daniel Pipes, The article concludes: "Although this line of research is discounted by Islamic traditionalists, Western scholars have generally applauded Crone and Cook's advances in tracing the origins of Islam." When I insisted that Wikipedia provide a source to support the above conclusion, the editor added "citation needed" to the conclusion. As of today, no citation to support the conclusion has been furnished.

Part of the confusion arises from the fact that Cook and Crone have made no manifest effort to repudiate their juvenile findings in the book. The authors admitted to me that they had not done it and cater no plans to do so. Repudiating scholarly work is not easy because sometimes errors are intertwined with valid findings. No scholar is obligated to rewrite books to correct errors. Scholarly decency, however, demands that the authors officially repudiate a scandalous thesis, one in which they no longer believe and one that maligns the faith of more than a billion people.

It appears however that the authors do not wish to discount a book that launched their careers and brought to them contacts and fortune. Patricia Crone teaches at the Institute for Advanced Studies, the academic home of Albert Einstein, an institute that proclaims itself as "one of the world's leading centers for theoretical research and intellectual inquiry." Michael Cook is a chaired professor of Near Eastern Studies at Princeton University, who in 2002 (a few months after 9/11 terrorist attacks) received $1.5 million Distinguished Achievement Award from the Mellon Foundation "for significant contribution to humanities research."

One needs no brains to write against Islam in the Western world. After 9/11, anti-Islamic literature has become a big business that even acclaimed academics have generously exploited for self-promotion. In this milieu, repudiating even a false anti-Islamic book will be condemned as apostasy. We need not burn the book. Crone and Cook themselves must muster the courage and put out the brushfire they started three decades ago, albeit in youthful excitement.

18. VENDING FUN

The United States House of Representatives has allocated more than a billion dollars for global broadcasting. The money will be used to internationalize American values, particularly in the Middle East where a new radio and television network would soon be launched. The US State Department is already sponsoring and subsidizing a new Arabic-language magazine, called Hi, to woo young Arabs to a new ideological viewpoint that America — regardless of its controversial and possibly failed foreign policy in the region — means well, is good at heart, and can be counted as a good reliable friend.

The masterminds of the Middle East broadcasting idea have called on Hollywood to plot the ways in which the lovely face of America's ruling elite can be projected with special effects. Responding to the mission bell, movie and advertising executives in California are scratching their heavy heads to create sitcoms, songs, cartoons, and images to persuade the Middle East's disgruntled youth that Washington DC is a lovely place, not to be hated and reviled but to be loved and revered.

If everything goes well, the broadcasting bonanza will fill a thousand Arabian nights, from Casablanca to Cairo to Dubai, with music, lifestyle choices, humor and political editorials. Don't be surprised if the voices of pretty girls and pretty boys wake up the Islamists in the middle of the night, not to call them to prayer but to whisper in their ears Welcome to the Hotel California — a most delicious American song of the counter-culture movement — a song truly magical if you hear it in a speeding Mercedes on a dark desert highway.

At the heart of all this — the radio, the television, the magazine — the message to be beamed will be loud and clear: Dear young Arabs are you looking for sweet summer, dance, or pink champagne on ice? Don't worry. You can find it here. By here we mean here in the Middle East, and not here in America. We urge you to fight to get these rights, but please, please do not rush to apply for an American visa for that shall be most certainly denied any time of year.

Of course, critics will poke fun at the idea of Hollywood propagating American values to the Middle East. They will be quick to point out how both Washington DC and Hollywood have glamorized violence in the real as well as the fantasized world. What is on TV is not America and what is America is not on TV, they would say.

Take the luminous bombing that lit up the skies of Baghdad. The designers conceived it as a shimmering light that would fuse shock with awe, image with reality, guilt with innocence. It was meant to be a show of lights. But then darkness fell. Now, American foot soldiers are being killed day after day, city by city. This is how, critics argue, Washington DC and Hollywood team up to fail America. But unruffled Rumsfeld has been found humming: I told you so. This could be Heaven or this could be Hell. But before you demonize the entire American civilization, relax and beware, that, away from Hollywood and Washington

DC, there is another America where ordinary folks indeed preserve and promote American values. You may not see them dance on TV, you may not hear them sing on radio and you may not read about them in the magazine, but they are there.

These ordinary Americans have no taste for aggression, nor do they appreciate occupation of any country. Even though America is a democracy and the people are presumably in charge of the government, they have little control over what Hollywood and Washington DC choose to do here in America or elsewhere. And before you run for the door, remember ordinary Americans do not hate Muslims, nor do they love them, they are just starting to study Islam, which in itself is remarkable. Soon after 9/11, the times were uncertain and it was no fun to be a Muslim. Yet, most Americans retained their composure and even goodwill.

Here in Kansas, good-hearted Americans visited our mosques to assure our safety, left messages of goodwill on phone machines, wrote notes of support, and even dropped money in the pail after the *Juma* prayer. This is the America you can check out any time you like but you can never leave...

19. SAVING CHRISTIANS

Aasia Bibi, a 45-year old Christian woman, has been sentenced to death, under Section 295-C of the Pakistan Penal Code, for allegedly 'defiling' the Prophet (PBUH). Though Aasia is the first woman to be convicted for blasphemy, Christians, Hindus and hundreds of Muslims have been charged under the statute.

Section 295 is a convenient legal tool to settle petty personal scores, intimidate rival families and practice ill-informed versions of Islam, particularly in small towns and villages. Local judges come under pressure to convict persons charged under the statute with the strident approval of local elders. Over the years, attempts to repeal the statute have provoked stiff opposition from Muslim jurists and invited threats of violence from militant groups. Even Pervez Musharraf, a secular military dictator, could not, for fear of imminent and severe reprisals, repeal the statute. For the same reasons, major political parties are disinclined to correct the blasphemy statute.

Recognizing the political difficulties of repealing the blasphemy statute or declaring it unconstitutional through judicial review, this legal commentary explores a different option. We ask that Pakistan's high courts build safety measures around the inherent faults of the blasphemy statute, particularly Section 295-C, which carries the death penalty.

More specifically, we argue that 295-C violates the due process clause of the Pakistan constitution and is repugnant to the Basic Code (the Quran and Sunnah), which, according to Article 227 of the constitution, is the supreme law of the land. In each case, including that of Aasia Bibi, the high courts must interpret and apply the blasphemy statute in ways consistent with the constitution and the Basic Code.

In 2010, Article 10 of the constitution was amended to introduce the due process clause into the criminal justice system. The amendment provides that a person charged with crime is entitled to due process. This due process clause applies to the blasphemy statute as well, securing civil rights in charges filed under 295-C. These protections now mandate more scrupulous applications of the blasphemy statute.

The over-broad language of 295-C punishes with death or life imprisonment any person who "by words, either spoken or written, or by visible representation or by any imputation, innuendo, or insinuation, directly or indirectly, defiles the sacred name of the Holy Prophet Muhammad." While the punitive part of the statute is lucid, the definition of blasphemy is vague and wide open. And the death penalty for prohibited speech is disproportionate, if not cruel and unusual.

A universal understanding of due process requires that criminal laws be drafted in a clear language for the average person to understand. The due process clause requires a clear and fair notice of criminality. This precision is even more crucial when a crime encroaches upon the right to free speech and to profess religion. The sweeping language of 295-C muddles protected speech with criminal speech.

Aasia Bibi was convicted for allegedly professing that Muhammad is not a prophet as are Abraham, Moses and Jesus. As a Christian, she believes that Abraham, Moses and Jesus are prophets. And as a Christian, she does not believe that Muhammad is God's Prophet. So what she professed was consistent with her core beliefs. No high court can ignore due process and confirm the death penalty of a Christian woman professing her faith. The blasphemy statute does not punish Muslims for denying that Jesus is son of God, a belief of Islam that could be offensive to Christians.

Pakistani high courts cannot apply the blasphemy statute shorn of due process and civil rights. Otherwise, 295-C is an unwary trap for persons such as Aasia and an unbridled source of power to those charged with enforcing its open-ended mandate. Simply put, 295-C violates fundamental due process rights of life, liberty and freedom of religion protected under the constitution. The courts must apply the blasphemy statute in ways consistent with defendants' fundamental rights.

Most importantly, the blasphemy statute is incompatible with Islamic law. Article 227 states: "All existing laws shall be brought in conformity with the Injunctions of Islam as laid down in the Holy Quran and Sunnah [Basic Code]." We submit that 295-C should be interpreted and applied in a manner not repugnant to the Basic Code. Religious minorities enjoy certain immutable rights under the Basic Code, which no positive law can take away.

First, religious minorities are free to practice religion even if their beliefs contradict the basics of Islam. The Quran reaffirms the principle that "there is no compulsion in matters of religion". An Islamic state's statute cannot dictate what non-Muslims should or should not believe, nor can it rely on capital punishment to silence other faiths.

Second, Pakistan as a Muslim state is obligated to

protect the life, liberty, property and dignity of religious minorities. When groups foment persecution of non-Muslims, the state must provide protection and security.

In his own life, the Prophet was verbally and physically abused. In most cases, he appeared forgiving and merciful. Of course, we are not suggesting that Pakistan should allow the defiling of the Prophet. Consistent with the Basic Code, we submit that Section 295-C must be reserved only for malicious attacks on the Prophet and even in such cases, the courts should know that the Basic Code prefers repentance and forgiveness over punishment.

20. TAKING CARE OF OLD AND FRAIL PARENTS

The Quran forbids Muslims from uttering even a small word of unkindness to their aging parents. In America, however, elder abuse is on the rise. Old and frail parents are left to rot in nursing homes; some live and die in wretched loneliness; some are cursed, ridiculed, kicked, and slapped by their own sons and daughters. Frightening stories of parental neglect and abuse are fracturing the moral foundation on which good old America is built.

The National Center on Elder Abuse, established by the US government, projects that by 2030, one in every five Americans would be sixty-five years or older. These demographic trends--bedeviled by an expensive healthcare system--will increase and compound incidences of elder abuse. For, old age accompanied by disease and disability invites neglect and abuse, particularly when the bond of compassion between parents and children is infirm.

Experts, who study the causes of domestic elder abuse, point out that many American families simply cannot bear the stress of taking care of the elderly. Driven by life's celerity, each member of the family pursues his or her own self-development and sees parental care as a drain on time and resources. Furthermore, children who have been neglected and abused develop the 'battered child grown old' syndrome. Under this syndrome, the abuser abuses the abuser, that is, sons and daughters neglect and abuse their feeble parents because the parents neglected and abused them when they were vulnerable children. This pathological relationship can be captured in a well-known American proverb: What goes around comes around.

To preempt these problems, the Quran's rules of parental care are rooted in a simple principle of 'kindness begets kindness.' Addressing all human beings (not just Muslims), and instructing them all to be good to their parents, the Quran (31:14) reminds sons and daughters how their parents took care of them when they were young and how their mothers protected them when they suffered from "weakness upon weakness." This reminder to grown-up sons and daughters presupposes that the parents have duly fulfilled their obligations toward children.

For, according to Islam, the normal dynamic of life is none else but reciprocity. Parents who were once sturdy become fragile, and children who were once weak become strong. This inevitable exchange of positions is sweetened with reciprocal kindness. Children savor a decent childhood as their parents provide tender and loving care, and parents enjoy a dignified old age as their children "lower onto them the wing" of protective kindness, and pray: "My Lord! Bestow on (my parents) Thy Mercy for they cherished me in childhood." (Quran 17:24). This reciprocal tenderness is the antithesis of the 'battered child grown old' syndrome.

One need not conclude, however, that the Quran subscribes to the behavior of tit for tat. The Islamic principle of reciprocity is fused with forgiveness and generosity. Muslims are obligated to take care of parents even if they disbelieve in Islam. And even if the parents have been neglectful in childcare, good Muslims shun the so-called syndrome of revenge against parents, nor do they forward the abuse to their own children. They end the cycle of abuse by means of forgiveness and generosity.

Although Islamic teachings of parental care are superb, it cannot be assumed that Muslim communities are free of elder neglect and abuse. The problem might be hidden because few victims come forward to tell their stories. Even in the United States, where mandatory reporting is legally required, only one out of eight cases of elder abuse is reported. Victims themselves do not report out of fear of retaliation and further neglect and abuse in both homes and nursing homes.

Just like the United States, Muslim countries must first study the problem of elder abuse to assess its scope and severity. Even though Islam protects members of the extended family, elderly Muslims without children are especially vulnerable. It would help if laws are enacted requiring that incidences of elder neglect and abuse be reported. Furthermore, the definition of elder abuse must be expanded beyond physical assault. It must also include financial exploitation and embezzlement of property, for relatives as caregivers can be wolves in the fleece of a sheep.

These legal measures are needed to enforce the teachings of Islam under which taking care of old and frail parents is not an optional *sawab* (reward) but a binding decree placed next to worshipping One God. "Your Lord had decreed that you worship none but Him, and that you be kind to parents." (Quran 17:23).

21. SOLVING PROBLEMS

Great nations possess keys that open and secure their advancement. Solving problems is one such key that has made America a successful nation. Muslims — though they have valid reasons to mistrust some American values — can nonetheless benefit by learning how Americans use problem-solving techniques in managing personal and public affairs.

Take the example of a leaking faucet. You have several options to respond. One, of course, is to live with the leaking faucet, day after day, not even recognizing it as a problem; or, you may acknowledge the faulty faucet but do nothing to halt its dripping. In a diagnostic style, you might fiddle with the faucet — knowing nothing about how faucets work — and jiggle it (softly or violently) in the vain hope that the problem would go away. Upon failing to stop the leak, you might find a solution in strangulating the faucet's neck with a piece of cloth. To nobody's surprise, the leaking faucet would not have been fixed. For most Americans, the most effective, efficient and durable solution would be calling a plumber (seeking professional help) to have the faucet fixed.

The American love affair with problem-solving is by no means limited to household plumbing. It cuts across the entire spectrum of personal and public life. Personal problems such as illness, debt, marital discord, and social problems such as clogged city traffic, load shedding in water, electricity or gas supplies, uncollected garbage, expanding crime — all are seen as problems for which solutions must be found. If a problem festers, more is done to reach its roots. Of course, America is not free of problems; perhaps, no society can ever be. In fact, some American problems, including lingering racism and escalating family breakdown, demonstrate that not even a mighty nation can solve all the problems.

Still, what distinguishes America among nations is the cultural emphasis placed on solving present and future problems through constant innovation. Nicholas Butler, an American educationist, compares the history of American nation-building with that of a futuristic laboratory that predicts and solves the problems of tomorrow. Prevention has always been the best cure of problems. But innovation in solving problems is the most dramatic dimension of American experience. Abraham Maslow, an American psychologist, has insightfully noted that if the only tool you have is a hammer, you might see every problem as a nail. Maslow's observation affirms that a major part of problem-solving is finding the right tools.

When old tools fail to fix problems, new tools must be invented. At the basic level, problem-solving is a human instinct. It is a human defense mechanism to adapt and adjust to the harsh realities of life. Yet the problem-solving instinct can be nurtured through instruction and training and turned into a skill. And the skill becomes a culture when individuals, families and governments, all are schooled in treating problems as barriers that must be removed. This problem-solving habit is now deeply ingrained in

American culture and can be seen in the study of law. The law of motor insurance for example is now oriented toward providing compensation to all injured in road accidents — a much better solution than wasting resources on finding fault. Most importantly, more than ninety percent of civil and criminal cases in America are settled, since negotiated solutions are found to be superior to litigated outcomes.

In borrowing problem-solving techniques from America, Muslims would be doing nothing contrary to the teachings of Islam. In fact, Islam requires sustained striving to solve national and personal problems. At the national level, the message is clear: God brings no change in the condition of a people unless the people themselves make an effort to bring the change (Quran 13:11). This message repudiates do-nothing reliance on divine forces to solve human problems, and proclaims self-help as a necessary tool for a progressive nation.

At the personal level, a call for solving problems and not living with them is repeatedly made. Consider health. *Sahih Bukhari* documents the Prophet's sayings that God has created a cure for every disorder and that Muslims are obligated to seek treatment for their illnesses. When he fell ill, the Prophet himself consulted physicians, and instructed others that taking care of one's health is the right of the human body. These instructions reject fatalism and the accompanying culture of doing nothing in face of adversity. Inspired by the teachings of Islam, Ibn Sina (Avicenna) searched secrets of the human body and penned *The Cannon of Medicine*, a masterpiece that remained for six centuries the sole authoritative medical book in the East and the West.

In locating solutions, as Ibn Sina's research confirms, Islam recommends the scientific method. Accordingly, Islam enjoins finding solutions derived from magic, palmistry, astrology or other speculative myths and fables. Even the use of high rhetoric is proscribed so that forceful speakers do not persuade the people into doing the wrong thing. Fact-based research expressed in simple, non-emotive language has been the most effective scientific method in solving human problems.

Consistent with the scientific method, Islam respects professional expertise. When the Prophet moved from Makkah to Medina, he prohibited Medina's date-growers from pollinating palm trees. As wind-assisted natural pollination is insufficient for commercial production, the yield of dates dropped the following year. Upon learning this, the Prophet ordered that man-assisted pollination be resumed, saying to the date-growers: "You have better knowledge (of a technical skill) in the affairs of the world."(*Sahih Muslim*/Trans. Abdul Hamid Siddiqi). This hadith clarifies that developing and respecting research-tested professional expertise are the most effective ways to solve problems and multiply benefit.

Relying on the scientific method, America has translated problem-solving principles into practical skills. Muslims need to do the same. The key is simple: First is the recognition of a problem; second is its accurate diagnosis; and, third is finding an effective, efficient, and durable solution. But to solve real life problems, Muslims must make a commitment to professionalism, vocational skills, and, most importantly, to nurturing a culture that takes pride in fixing problems rather than living with them. A culture of solving problems is established when individuals develop practical skills in specific areas and stop acting as experts on every topic under discussion.

22. REFINING JOURNALISM

For several months, I have been watching Pakistani talk shows, including Capital Talk, Kal Tak, Islamabad Tonight, and Tonight with Moeed Pirzada. These and other talk shows invite ministers, politicians, journalists, and sometimes experts to discuss national matters concerning foreign policy, domestic governance, terrorism, and prominent legal cases before the Supreme Court. These shows, though aired at different TV channels, follow a formulaic pattern in that each talk show has an anchor and each talk show, aired four or five times a week, invites three or four panelists to discuss a specific topic for nearly an hour. The talk shows provide irrefutable evidence that the Pakistani media is free, perhaps freer than the corporatist media in the United States. However, the Pakistani talk shows, though exuberant, are for the most part crude, unruly, and uneducated, potentially as detrimental to the dissemination of quality ideas as are the savvy but highly filtered talk shows in the U.S. corporatist media.

The Pakistani talk shows, conducted in Urdu with generous interspersion of English phrases, are seemingly framed for the educated classes of Pakistan, aimed particularly at Islamabad policymakers, with the hope that the government, the army, the parliament, and the judiciary would watch these shows to grasp problems and find solutions. The shows might also be seeking to educate the general public. Unfortunately, most talk shows fail in their reformist and educational mission because many panelists are poorly informed and many anchors are poorly prepared for the topic of the day to deliver a fruitful conversation.

Poorly-Informed Panelists

The talk shows noticeably vary in quality depending on the knowledge and expertise of anchors and panelists. For the most part, however, the talk shows summon the same few politicians and media analysts regardless of the topic. Some days, the same politicians rotate from one show to the other improvising opinions on topics as varied as the shortage of energy, causes of terrorism, and the culture of corruption. Many panelists have no credible expertise to discuss the given topics with any helpful knowledge or beneficial information. Most panelists, including media analysts and lawyers, engage in shouting matches, all talking at the same time, adding little to the discussion but clichés, party slogans, hackneyed jokes, and sensational accusations against each other. The anchors, enjoying the verbal brawl among panelists, further downgrade the poor quality of discussion by provoking guests against each other.

The poor quality of talk shows reveals a profound truth about the Pakistan culture. For decades, the Pakistani culture has tolerated a norm that each person is qualified to render opinions on any topic. It is culturally alien for a Pakistani to say sorry I don't know anything about this topic. Consequently, the culture allows everyone to express opinions on any topic, including how an F-16 flies, what is the most effective treatment for leukemia, or why cars can or cannot be fueled with water. The freedom to express opinions is a fundamental liberty protected under the law of human rights. While Pakistan must be appreciated for turning this freedom into a cultural artifact, the truth remains that not everyone knows how an F-16 flies. Ad-libbing is fun and cathartic, but opinions expressed in educational shows will be far more beneficial if founded on sound knowledge. It is therefore necessary for talk show managers to fight the cultural norm of I-know-it all and carefully select panelists who have the relevant knowledge and expertise on a given topic. Most importantly, the talk shows must diversify the list of panelists and choose competence over convenience in choosing guests.

Poorly-Prepared Anchors

Even though the talk-show industry is nascent in Pakistan, some anchors have developed impressive professional skills to conduct interviews and pose sharp questions. The anchor of Jirga, for example, is a consummate interviewer. His recent interview with Afghanistan President Hamid Karzai was superb and professionally done. The anchor of Aapas Ki Baat is mostly well-prepared and conducts a polite but instructive dialogue. By contrast, the hosts of Bolta Pakistan rarely use their airtime effectively and come across as rude and clownish, engaging in fruitless diatribe.

One defect that mars most shows is the anchors' inadequate preparation. It is no secret that behind every successful anchor is a competent team that researches and prepares the topic materials and coaches the anchor for conducting a meaningful conversation with well-informed experts. In the United States, the PBS News Hour is a good example of a well-informed show where each anchor prepares for a small segment of the program with the help of research staff. It appears that the Pakistani TV channels do not provide anchors with sufficient resources and research assistance to prepare for the show. A talk show is rarely effective when an ill-prepared anchor engages in a dialogue with poorly-informed guests.

The other defect in Pakistani talk shows is high frequency in that the same anchor conducts four or five full-length shows every week. Capital Talk, for example, is aired at least four times a week. Even though its anchor is a respected media person, he does not get sufficient time to prepare for each show. Most anchors conducting four or five shows a week are rarely well-prepared for the various topics they undertake to discuss. The quality of discussion plummets when a poorly-prepared anchor, instead of facilitating a conversation among panelists, begins to assert his own combative viewpoints. I have seen anchors, not lawyers by training, who boldly interpret the Pakistan constitution to refute the constitutional lawyers invited on the panel.

Conclusion

The Pakistani talk shows aired at various TV channels are designed to educate the public and influence the policymakers in Islamabad. The mission is laudable and should not be abandoned. These shows, however, fail in their mission because most panelists lack the relevant knowledge and expertise to discuss the topics. An anchor conducting four or five full-length shows a week simply does not have adequate prep time to research the topic and conduct a useful dialogue. These shows can be effective if TV channels provide competent research staff to coach the anchor and cut down the weekly frequency of a show from four to one or two. Also, the talk show managers need to expand the roster of national, regional, and international experts in various fields and refrain from inviting the same few persons over and over again.

Freedom of press is a great principle of modern civilization and it is needed in all Muslim nations regardless of the form of government. Censorship breeds cruelty and corruption. However, media houses must hire talented journalists committed to fair and accurate reporting within the ethics of Islam and canons of journalism. .

23. ADOPTING CLEANLINESS

Now for more than a century, cleanliness has been a profound American value. This value is manifested in both personal and public hygiene. The American story of hygiene transformation has great lessons for the rest of the world, particularly for the Islamic world.

For most Americans, personal hygiene comes first. They take daily showers, shampoo their hair, use deodorants to suppress sweating, manicure their nails, and keep their mouths fresh; women go regularly to beauty parlors, men prune themselves mostly at home. Personal grooming is prompted by a desire to be clean as well as by an impulse to look nice -- for the American culture of cleanliness has come to appreciate good looks -- though painted with the brush of narcissism.

A fusion of cleanliness and good looks is not confined to personal grooming. It is also visible in homes and public places. Government buildings, corporate offices, schools, hospitals, and shopping malls are clean. An additional effort is made to make them look pleasant and beautiful. Flowers, trees, plants, and decorations highlight entrances, hallways, and common areas. Just like grooming a human face, a lot is contemplated and done to improve the looks of public buildings.

Good-looking public places, however, are not mere faces without substance. Real efforts are made to safeguard genuine cleanliness, for public hygiene is the science of preserving the health of the community. In most American counties and cities, therefore, local governments make sure that water is available and safe to drink, and that garbage and sewage are properly removed from streets and factories. Americans have learned that municipal housekeeping requires political action. And it also needs the expertise of skilled engineers and town planners who must carefully plan water and sewage systems. Air pollution is a more complex problem that, above all, requires cooperation of the industry.

No government, however, can maintain public hygiene unless the people cooperate. Ordinary Americans do. They do not trash roads, parks, parking lots, or other common areas. Except for some baseball players, very few Americans spit in public.

But Americans were not always like this. In her remarkable book, *Chasing Dirt: The American Pursuit of Cleanliness* (Oxford, 1995), Suellen Roy traces the history of how America has changed from dreadfully dirty to clean. Before the American Civil War (1860s), she writes, men spat everywhere, flies accompanied every meal, foul smells emanated from everywhere, hundreds of roaming pigs scavenged garbage thrown into thoroughfares, there was no running water and no plumbing. Of the American habit of chewing and spitting tobacco, Charles Dickens found this filthy custom inseparably mixed with all the transactions of social life. For the most part, the author of Chasing Dirt concludes, the American cities and towns were dirty and dangerous.

After the Civil War, however, American leaders began to advocate personal cleanliness as a moral and patriotic value. It became un-American to be dirty, regardless of the nature of work. New immigrants were taught English and hygiene. Dirt was no longer touted as the worker's jewelry. It was now associated with disease. Epidemics such as cholera and yellow fever brought home the liaison between filth and death. The fear of disease and death, coupled with vigorous education about the benefits of personal hygiene, persuaded Americans to reform their personal habits.

But personal hygiene was not enough to fix the macro problem. Something had to be done to clean cities and communities. Committed sanitarians harped on a simple thesis that uncollected garbage was the greatest nuisance. They lobbied with the government for laying sewers and with the people to install plumbing in houses. Indoor plumbing and outdoor sewers became America's obsession. Resources and political will were brought together to enforce the ethic of cleanliness. With an unprecedented vigor and commitment, America was changing from a dirty nation to a world-class model of personal and public hygiene.

Purification is a profound Islamic value. In Islam, cleanliness is a religious duty. The mandatory wudu (ablution) before daily prayers -- for no prayer is accepted without it -- is a practical lesson in personal hygiene that all Muslims internalize from childhood. Wudu cleans hands, arms, nostrils, mouth, and feet -- all the limbs exposed to dirt. Furthermore, Muslims are required to wash private parts after answering the call of nature, a value not yet American. And if water is available, the Quran mandates ghusl (taking a bath), particularly after sexual intercourse. While taking a bath, the prophet recommended that the hair be thoroughly washed; and he was fond of taking scented baths (Bukhari). Thus, we see that personal hygiene constitutes a core value of the Islamic faith.

While most Muslims are clean in their bodies, some Islamic communities are dirty. Indoor plumbing is still unavailable in many cities and villages. Adults urinate and children defecate wherever they can or want to. We go to masjids in clean clothes but remain unsure whether we will get there clean, for the road to the masjid is often strewn with raw sewage and flying garbage. Visitors are not going to think highly of our great religion if Muslim cities and communities are dreadfully dirty.

The American story of Chasing Dirt tells us that if a nation is determined to obtain public hygiene, it can achieve dramatic results. But to do so, everyone-- government, businesses, neighborhoods, charities, families, and individuals--has to join the jihad to enforce cleanliness throughout the Islamic world. This should be done not for one time cleaning but for establishing a culture of public and personal hygiene. As I am finishing writing this article, I receive an email from Topeka Corporate Volunteer Council. In sponsoring the Operation Sweep Clean, we are gathering products here on campus that will be distributed to organizations such as the Rescue Mission, Doorstep, and Let's Help. Products needed are soap, shampoo, toothpaste or any personal care items. The donation boxes will be in every building. The email confirmed my belief that cleanliness is a constant jihad.

Taking the faith seriously and marshalling the necessary will and resources, Islamic countries can and must be clean and good-looking, for "Allah is beautiful and loves beauty.".

24. PROTECTING PUBLIC PROPERTY

Pakistanis are one of the most generous peoples of the world and many go out of their way to share what little they have with relatives, friends, and even strangers. Miserliness is culturally reproached as it is condemned in their religion. Despite these noteworthy qualities, Pakistanis have little respect for public property, that is, the natural and human-made properties accessible to all members of the society. Unfortunately, the people of Pakistan trash parks, roads, rivers, lakes, beaches, forests, government buildings; they also steal from public utilities, such as Water and Power Development Authority (WAPDA), Pakistan Railways (PR), and Pakistan International Airlines (PIA). This lack of respect for public property reinforces corruption that runs through every artery of the Pakistani economy. Politicians, bureaucrats, retired army officers, and even ordinary persons, all are inclined to misuse and misappropriate public properties one way or the other. As a result, public properties are grimy, unkempt, dysfunctional, inefficient, and furrowed with pandemic greed and self-interest.

In 2012, Pakistan scored a meager 27 points out of 100 in the Corruption Perceptions Index, trailing many Muslim and regional nations. Unless the cultural habit of trashing and pilfering public property is transformed, Pakistan will remain a mucky, problematic, and poorly managed country. Without cultivating genuine respect for public property, no form of democracy and no economic planning, no matter how sound in theory, will succeed in solving the shortage of energy, water, and other chronic problems associated with Pakistan's public properties.

Trashing Public Property

While most Pakistanis maintain their individual houses studiously, they turn around and trash public property without any guilt or mercy. Throwing the household garbage out on the street is still the popular method that the people use in many neighborhoods, a practice that poses serious health risks. Trash in the form of garbage, plastic bags, hospital waste, and raw sewage befouls roads, parks, rivers, and other public spaces. While waste generation is on the rise, waste management is non-existent in most towns and villages. Poorly designed waste management systems frequently break down in big cities including Lahore and Karachi.

The people, showing utter disrespect for public property, adopt non-cooperative behaviors that undermine garbage disposal systems. Municipalities employ thoughtless methods for waste collection. It is common to see uncovered garbage trucks and trolleys, littering streets as much as collecting litter, eventually causing outbreaks of cholera and malaria. The practice of burning garbage in open spaces produces toxic gasses that pollute the environment. Every year, Pakistan produces thousands of engineers and even exports them to foreign countries. Yet, no credible effort goes into designing waste management systems that would effectively collect and dispose of household and industrial garbage. Incompetence and indifference wreck public properties seething with foul odors, flies, and insects, ravaging public health.

Pilfering Public Property

Much more than trashing, pilfering public property is Pakistan's chronic social behavior. Misappropriating, embezzling, and outright stealing public property define the national character of this nation comprised of, ironically, religiously conservative people. Take electricity, an asset placed in the public sector. Electricity worth millions of dollars is stolen each year because a powerful mafia sponsors the electricity theft. The PR and the PIA, the two transportation giants in the public sector, are the prime examples of theft and corruption. Politicians and bureaucrats who negotiate locomotive and aircraft deals take kickbacks and end up buying faulty equipment requiring expensive maintenance costs. Locomotives and aircrafts frequently break down causing delays and cancellations of trains and flights. The President of Pakistan, notorious for taking kickbacks and known in the whole world as Mr. Ten Percent, captures the moral tragedy of a nation that can trust no one in power to protect public properties from thieves.

Kleptomania is not confined to the ruling elites. Even ordinary people pilfer public property. The people steal iron bars, bricks, and even concrete blocks laid in bridges, roadways, and waterways. The theft of drain and sewer manhole covers is a common criminal activity. In Islamabad, the nation's capital, young and old thieves armed with hammers and crowbars come out at night, break open the iron covers sealed with cement, and sell them the next day in the scrap market. The uncovered manholes located in the middle of roads and sidewalks trap motor vehicles and pedestrians, causing injury and death.

Of all ills, tax theft is the most significant factor that undermines Pakistan's fragile economy. First, very few people pay taxes including income tax, sales tax, excise duty, or customs duty. The rich and the powerful find legal and illegal ways for tax avoidance and tax exemptions. The lawmakers themselves rarely file tax returns, even though most of them are wealthy. Second, revenue officers take bribes to unlawfully lower taxpayers' liability. In every revenue department, businesses and individuals find illegal ways to evade or reduce taxes. No taxation without representation, a political slogan of the American Revolution, is well known in Pakistan. However, Pakistan has yet to learn a more fundamental concept that a nation without taxation disintegrates.

Conclusion

The people of Pakistan need to understand that no nation can survive, let alone thrive, unless its people safeguard public property. Political and religious leaders, the media, teachers in schools and universities, and parents, all have first to teach themselves and then to others that public property, be it rivers, lakes, beaches, roads, railways, airlines, or utilities, is a sacred trust that one generation passes to the next, preferably with improvements. When public property is trashed and pilfered, the people are deprived of essential services critical for living a normal life and raising families. And in this process of trashing and thieving the nation loses its moral character...

25. CONFEDERATED BATTLEFIELDS

A potentially perilous pattern of militancy is developing in response to the Western war on terror. Muslim militants across the world are confederating to assist each other. A few days after the French forces attacked Mali militants, a band of Muslim militants captured Western workers at an Algerian natural gas complex owned by British and Norwegian oil companies. While the French soldiers, receiving assistance from the Germans and the British, were killing Muslim militants in Mali, Muslim militants of various nationalities were threatening to kill Western hostages at the Algerian gas complex. This is not the first time Muslim militants have confederated to counter Western attacks. The Taliban of Pakistan and the Taliban of Afghanistan, along with Arabs, Chechens, and others, reinforce each other in fighting Western troops. The philosophy of al Qaeda, the mother of modern militancy, privatizes military jihad but also unites Muslim militants of all national stripes into a confederation. As the West aggregates its resources to collectively fight Muslim militants whether they are in Afghanistan, Mali, or elsewhere, Muslim militants are similarly confederating to fight the West at various hotspots. Increasingly, Muslim militancy mirrors and reciprocates the Western combat policy.

Western Combat Policy

It is no secret that the Western nations have developed a highly coordinated combat policy to fight unfriendly rulers and militants in the Muslim world, a fact that does not go unnoticed among militancy circles. For example, the United States, Canada, Western Europe, and Australia, all joined forces to fight al Qaeda and overthrow the Taliban government in Afghanistan. The NATO combat mission to kill Muammar Gaddafi, an entrenched Arab ruler who sponsored militancy for decades, was highly coordinated among the key Western powers. Earlier, the Western combat mission to remove Saddam Husain, without approval of the U.N. Security Council, was coordinated among the United States, the United Kingdom, Australia, and Poland, the nations that supplied troops for the invasion of Iraq. The continuing combat mission to unseat Bashar Assad of Syria, despite the opposition of China and Russia, has been hatched, funded, and supported by Western nations. The French attack on Mali militants is by no means a mere colonial intervention by a lone state. Germany, the United Kingdom, and Canada are providing logistical support and ideological legitimacy to the combat mission. The Western combat policy to nullify the Iranian clerical rule is not yet successful but the policy persists at the expense of inflicting intolerable pain on the Iranian people.

The Western combat policy, framed as a national security paradigm, is gathering legitimacy in part because Muslim rulers, mostly undemocratic, and many of whom despise each other, are more than willing to endorse, and sometimes solicit, Western invasions and targeted assassinations in Muslim lands. The U.S. drone attacks in Pakistan and Yemen are perpetrated with the approval of local and regional governments. The governments of Morocco and Algeria opened their airspace for the French aircrafts to fly through and attack Mali militants. Some Muslim governments are assisting the Western nations in overthrowing Syria's Bashar Assad and undermining Iran's clerical rule. Unfortunately, the Organization of Islamic Conference (OIC), an inter-governmental organization of 57 Muslim states, has been unable to unite the Muslim world into any meaningful union. Trapped in leadership frictions and the Shia-Sunni strains, the OIC member states could not develop effective strategies to control militancy, democratize political systems, protect human rights, and defend Muslim lands against foreign assaults. Almost every Muslim state is confronting internal militancy.

Furthermore, a perception reigns among militancy circles that the West has employed myriad international institutions to undergird its combat policy. The International Criminal Court (ICC), located in the Netherlands, is viewed as a choking tool to strangulate Muslim rulers who might oppose the Western combat policy. This view is strengthened when the ICC prosecutors declare the defiant Muslim rulers as international criminals. Similarly, the U.N. Security Council, with three Western states as its permanent members, is viewed as a premier international body that conceives, formulates, and enforces cruel economic sanctions against Muslim communities. The superior economic power of Western nations, asserted through the International Monetary Fund and the World Bank, is viewed as economic hegemony that snares many Muslim states into huge debts and the attendant dependence. Everything the West does in relation to the Muslim world is seen as yet another phase in a grand but ugly conspiracy.

Confederated Battlefields

The perception of an ever-tightening Western noose around unfriendly Muslim rulers, communities, and nations, does not deter but provokes the Islamic concept of military jihad. The siege mentality supplies the catalyst for Muslim militants to "fight and kill the disbelievers wherever you find them, take them captive, harass them, lie in wait and ambush them using every stratagem of war." Unless the Quran is expunged from human memory, something impossible, Muslim militants will continue to draw inspiration from their holy book to engage in military jihad. True, Islam is a peaceful religion but only in peaceful times. Islam is not a pacifist but a martial religion that carries a vigorous law of war. Because there is no one religious or temporal authority that controls the Muslim world, the military jihad is more and more manifested through confederated battlefields.

Under the Islamic law of war, a call for military jihad is mandatory when (a) a Muslim community is under siege; (b) the ruler is unable to vacate the siege through peaceful means; (c) the enemy is identifiable, and; (d) the oppression is intolerable. Under these conditions, the enemy's superior might is a non-factor. The classical rule of Islamic law requires that the Muslim ruler declare military jihad. This requirement, however, is no longer operational because the Muslim world is too large, too fragmented, many Muslim militants are poorly educated in the Islamic law of war, and many Muslim rulers as well as Islamic scholars are seen as foreign puppets rather than authentic leaders and jurists. Hence, the militancy circles scattered in the Muslim world conduct their own analyses, devise their own strategies, obtain their own weapons, and open battlefields of their own choosing. The confederated battlefields may or may not follow the Islamic law of war. The killing of non-combatant civilians and destroying places of worship, among other things, are strictly prohibited. Regrettably, the violations of Islamic law are multiplying.

Conclusion

The Western combat policy to punish and kill hostile Muslim rulers and militants, undermine unfriendly Muslim governments, and impose stiff economic sanctions on Muslim communities does not deter but provokes Muslim militants to engage in military jihad. Muslim militants fighting in various battlefields see the Western states as a monolithic enemy. They support each other's cause, duplicating the Western combat policy. The West and Muslim militancy are interlocked in a spiral of violence, threatening international peace and security. There has to be a way out other than more violence.

26. SUFIS AND TERROR

Armed with explosive belts and masked in headscarves, Chechen feminists and their Muslim brothers raided and captured a Moscow theater in late October. They threatened to kill some 700 hostages (mostly Russians, and some foreigners) who had come to the theater to enjoy *Nord Ost* – Russia's first home-grown, Western-style musical, highlighting failed brotherhood, missed opportunities, death and patriotism. The Chechens said they would kill their hostages unless Russian troops withdrew from Chechnya.

The occupation of the Moscow Theater, the Russian security forces' use of gas to end the siege, and the deaths of all the Chechens and over 100 hostages add more layers to an already complicated Russian war. Russian President Vladimir Putin, a former KGB Boss, apologized to his people for the casualties in the (unprecedented) rescue operation, but warned Chechans that his government would not succumb to terrorist blackmail (i.e. Chechnya will not be freed).

Possessing superior weapons and the will to kill,

successive Russian regimes of the Czars, Stalin, Yeltsin, and Putin have tried hard to put down the Muslim rebellion (dream for independence) in this physically rugged, psychologically stubborn, and spiritually indomitable region. In the 18th and 19th centuries, the Czars and Czarinas, including Catherine the Great, liquidated hundreds of thousands of the Chechens, but failed to pacify the resistance. In 1756, eighty percent of all the mosques in the region were destroyed, and the Chechens were forced to abandon Islam. Some did, most did not.

During the Second World War, Stalin accused the Chechens of colluding with the Germans. Along with others, 600,000 Chechens were deported to Serbia and Central Asia to do hard labor. The ill and the elderly were pushed out of the exile trains; many perished in the wilderness. Stalin ordered that Chechnya be removed from the official map of the Soviet Union, a move to deny Chechnya's separate existence. This official erasure did not last long, however, and Chechnya was soon put back on the official map as an autonomous region. In Chechnya, the bitter memories of deportation and death nonetheless survived, deepening the scars as well as the collective will to seek independence from Russia.

Freedom for Chechnya did not come even in 1991 when the Soviet Union collapsed as a nation-state and fell from the status of a super-power. The majority of 48 million Muslims were freed from the Soviet Union, but not the Chechens and the Kazan Tatars, the so-called internal Muslims. Boris Yeltsin, a democratically elected Russian President, waged a war against the Chechens to demand their allegiance to the Russian Federation and, incidentally, to secure Chechnya's substantial oil reserves). When the world community objected to Yeltsin's wanton use of force, Yeltsin responded with a well-known, though no longer valid international cliché: This is our internal affair. Yeltsin refused to negotiate with the Chechen bandits and vowed their complete destruction.

The world quietly listened to these threats of genocide, as if delivered in a musical -- though President Clinton, at a leadership conference, once hugged Yeltsin and reminded him how the world did not dismiss it as an internal affair but cheered for Russia's freedom when Yeltsin stood up on the tank in Moscow, in open defiance to the authorities in the Kremlin. But Yeltsin did not change his mind. When he eventually left the stage, he handed over his cue cards to President Putin.

In the past few years, though the war with Chechnya lingers, the set has changed. Before, the war was *in* Chechnya. Now the war is *with* Russia. Instead of fighting the war in Grozny, the capital of Chechnya, the Chechens have brought the war to Moscow, the capital of Russia. Before, according to Russia, the war in Chechnya was an internal affair; now, according to Russia, the war by the Chechens is part of an international crusade of Muslim terrorists. Before, the United States criticized the Russian use of force against the Chechens; now, it understands. Before, the liberation movement in Chechnya was anchored in the right to self-determination; now, it is a terrorist enterprise (the occupier has won the battle of labels). Before, Russia condemned Islam as a backward religion that oppresses women; now, Russia accuses Islam of turning Muslim women into heartless warriors. Before, the cause of terror was Islamic fundamentalism (Afghanistan); now it is Sufism (Chechnya).

Though Islamic theologians have been suspicious of the cult of the Sufis, the Chechans (and others in the region) converted to Islam thanks to the Sufis' personal power, not the sword. In Chechnya, scores of Sufi tombs serve as pilgrimage sites, where the Chechans go to renew their spiritual strengths. The Soviets admitted the vitality of Sufi shrines in Chechnya, but President Putin is considering how he might completely liquidate all cult structures in the mountains which serve as hiding places for the bandits. Following tradition, the Chechen Sufis teach love, reconciliation and forgiveness. However, Chechen Sufism has in recent centuries adopted militancy, at least since the first massive Russian aggression in 1785. The Chechen resistance then was led by a Sufi, known as Shaykh Mansur Ushurma. Declaring jihad, the Sufi and his men crushed the Czarist forces. Ever since, Chechen Sufism has mixed and matched the elements of resistance - peace with war, the veil with the gun.

Back at the theater, the suffocating deaths in Moscow raise a thousand questions. Does the play have a deeper plot when the innocent viewers do not come home alive? Is it Sufi militancy or sheer terror that has brought the war to Moscow? Are the Chechen bandits members of the Al-Qaeda, though the former have been around for centuries? Were the veiled women dressed in explosives just amateur actors, determined to kill the innocent audience of *Nord Ost*, or were they a new breed of Muslim women, determined to fight oppression and occupation? And then there is a more general question: What is it about Islam that prepares its followers to collide with mighty earthly powers? But of all the questions, one persists: What should one conclude when Sufis, saints and poets threaten to kill the innocent?

27. TAKFIRIZATION

Small-minded versions of Islam have fanaticized Pakistan - an antediluvian land with deep interfaith roots leavened with the teachings of Hindu Swamis, Buddhist Monks, Sikh Gurus, and Muslim Sufis - into a ghastly country. Stories are frightening. Few days ago, a native Christian couple, accused of desecrating the Qur'an, was thrown into a brick kiln and burned alive while a crowd of over a thousand villagers participated in the rite. In 2010, two Ahmadi mosques in Lahore were attacked with guns and grenades, killing 94 people. Around 5000 Hindus leave the Sindh province of Pakistan every year as their holy books and temples are burnt. Hindu women are abducted, forcibly converted to Islam, and married off to the kidnappers. Non-Muslims are not the only victims of hateful fanaticism. Muslim on Muslim violence is also escalating as Shias kill Sunnis and Sunnis kill Shias.

Behind religious violence in Pakistan is the rise of Takfiri (تكفيري) mindset, which sees Islam through a narrow keyhole of self-righteousness and accuses the world of apostasy.

Takfiri Mindset

Declaring others as deviants from "the one true divine path" is a universal phenomenon, found in all religions. In Islam, Takfiris are the self-appointed guardians of "true Islam." Takfiris proclaim that Muslims who do not follow a specific version of Shariah are Kafirs (non-believers), and not Muslims. They oppose the spiritually generous viewpoint that many paths lead to God and that there could be honest diversity within the same religion. Militant Takfiris use violence to enforce "true Islam." Ahmadis, Shias, and even Sufi-Sunnis are ambushed and killed because these groups, according to Takfiris, have corrupted "true Islam." Sufi shrines are bombed as places set against Shariah.

Ironically, Takfiris opposed the 1947 partition of India and saw Pakistan, a country acquired in the name of Islam, as a deviant nation. Most Pakistanis at the time of partition were highly pluralist who respected other sects and religions. For centuries, even after the arrival of Islam in the eight century, the spiritual folklore in Punjab and Sindh has emphasized love and compassion for all. Pakistan, long before its establishment, has been the love-land of Lal Shahbaz Qalandar (1177-1274), Guru Nanak (1469-1539), Shah Hussain (1538-1599), Sultan Bahu (1630-1691), Bulleh Shah (1680-1757), Latif Bhittai (1689-1752), and Waris Shah (1722-1798).

Gradually, Pakistan has been metamorphosed into Takfiri hatred. The Takfiris in Pakistan have become more assertive and influential. First, they have turned anti-India to gain legitimacy with the patriotic armed forces. Second, they have opened hundreds of primary schools to teach their "true Islam" to children, including Afghan refugees. Third, they promote the ideology that Pakistan was carved out of India for the sole divine purpose of advancing "true Islam" in the Subcontinent and beyond.

The Soviet invasion of Afghanistan and the

concomitant arrival of Saudi-Wahhabi puritanism further strengthened the Takfiri mindset. Even though the Wahhabi movement has failed to win the hearts and minds of Pakistanis, the Takfiri mindset is gathering motion and momentum. Fighting the Soviet infidels opened the floodgates of fighting all infidels. Self-righteousness is replacing spiritual plurality. The Takfiri mindset now argues that only "true Islam" belongs to Pakistan. Other religions and sects have no place in Pakistan. Hindus and Sikhs belong to India, Christians belong to the West, Shias belong to Iran, and Ahmadis are the infidels to be killed or converted to "true Islam."

Takfiri Laws

The Takfiri mindset has successfully entered the Constitution and laws of Pakistan. Note again that the Takfiris exclude certain believers from the realm of Islam. Article 260(3) of the Constitution provides the Takfiri definition of Islam, declaring Christians, Hindus, Sikhs, Buddhists, Parsis, Ahmadis, and Bahais to be "non-Muslims." Except for Ahmadis and Bahais, the Constitution seems to be underscoring the obvious. Yet, the constitutional emphasis on the definition of "non-Muslims" promotes social ostracization of religious minorities. Article 260(3) also gainsays the Qur'an, which states that Abraham, Moses, David, Noah, and Jesus were all Muslims. While the Qur'an expands the definition of Islam, the Takfiris restrict it to their warped musings.

In theory, Pakistan's blasphemy laws protect all religions. Chapter XV of the Pakistan Penal Code lays out offenses relating to religion. Article 295 of the Chapter prohibits defiling "any place of worship" and insulting "the religion of any class of persons." However, most other laws in the Chapter are consistent with the Takfiri mindset. Article 298-A opens the door for the persecution of the Shias who might not subscribe to the Sunni views about the First Four Caliphs and the Prophet's companions.

Article 298-C singles out the Ahmadis for criminal punishments if they pose as Muslims or refer to their faith as Islam. Articles 295-B and 295-C provide the harshest punishments for whoever (Hindus and Christians) is accused of disrespecting the Qur'an or the Prophet of Islam.

Encountering Takfiris

Since its establishment in 1947, Pakistan has been moving away from its time-tested traditions of universal love toward the troubling creed of targeted hatred. Tolerance, compassion, pluralism, diversity, forgiveness, kindness, and sweetness are no longer the supreme values of Islam, a great world religion. The Takfiri mindset of exclusion, persecution, and hard-heartedness is poisoning the cultures and communities of Punjab, Sindh, Balochistan, and Khyber-Pakhtunkhwa. The Takfiri mindset will further drive Pakistan into poverty, violence, sectarian warfare, and international isolation. The people of Pakistan, its intellectuals, teachers, political leaders, lawmakers, judges, lawyers, journalists, and the media houses need to wake up and begin to encounter the Takfiri mindset. .

28. BEYOND RELIGIONS

Humanity is taking a quantum leap beyond the religions of the world. Emerging from this quantum leap is a universal spirituality (USP) that removes ideological, gnostic, denominational, and sectarian borders within and across religions. Universal spirituality does not nullify the teachings of any religion, nor does it denigrate any faith or creed. The USP incorporates the morals derived from religions into shared consciousness. It respects the practices of each creed.

Churches, temples, synagogues, gurdwaras and mosques are the places of worship, tranquility, and goodness. The divine books, including Upanishads, Dhammapada, the Bible, the Qur'an, and the Granth Sahib, which animate old and new religions, constitute the heritage of humanity. The places of pilgrimage, including Benares, Jerusalem, Makkah and Black Hills, all are sacred repositories of shared reflection. Yogis, Sufis, monks, rabbis, priests, ministers and Imams, all are the guardians of spiritual traditions.

The USP does not exclude any religion, faith or creed,

from the realm of truth or authenticity. Consistent with the moral evolution of the human species, the USP interfuses the human psyche with cosmic intelligence, promoting the free flow of spirituality in and beyond space and time.

Goodness

The USP defines spirituality as goodness to oneself and to others. Dishonest, deceitful and miserly individuals cannot be spiritual no matter how much education or knowledge they accumulate. Likewise, nations and communities rife with violence, torture and enforced disappearances are tracking far away from the spiritual path. A people that occupy another people cannot be spiritual. Social systems that endorse racism, caste system or misogyny cannot be spiritual. Economic systems that promote material acquisitiveness and egotistical self-assertions may produce wealth but bring no spiritual joy for the participants. The USP establishes the principle of goodness as the bedrock of spirituality. Spirituality is not mere higher consciousness, it is not mere worship, and it is not mere remembering God. Spirituality is goodness to oneself and to others, pure and simple.

Creed Exceptionalism

The USP repudiates creed exceptionalism. No religion is superior to any other religion. And no religion has exceptional monopoly over truth or spiritual truth. Each religion lays out a spiritual path, good and authentic for its followers. As long as there are sincere followers of a religion, the religion cannot be suppressed. There is no external definition of religion. All religions are internal to the followers. Only weak spiritual traditions are intolerant of other religions. Universal spirituality allows the followers of each and every religion and denomination to freely practice their faith without harassment, criticism and denigration from the followers of another religion or from non-believers. The USP prohibits the burning of divine books or making fun of any prophets held in esteem by a religious community. It guides both believers and non-believers in taking the quantum leap and shunning the orbit of self-righteousness and prejudice.

Quiet and Personal Spirituality

Because universal spirituality rejects creed exceptionalism, it also rejects the principle of proselytization. The institution of proselytization emanates from creed exceptionalism, with the belief that the proselytizer practices a more truthful creed. Conversion from one faith to another is a personal choice, freely available under universal spirituality. However, criminalization of voluntary conversion is an abomination; and forced conversion is an ugly contravention of universal spirituality. Even artful proselytization obtained by offering material benefits is offensive to universal spirituality. The very notion of proselytization and "saving" presupposes that the creed of the person to be saved is erratic or inferior. Universal spirituality prohibits proselytization from one religion to another, from disbelief to belief, or from belief to disbelief. Each human being is entitled to quiet and personal spirituality without a knock at the door from state officials, intolerant neighbors or wandering proselytizers...

29. SUFI SPIRITUALITY

In 2012, a militant group wielding crude shovels and pickaxes damaged the ancient Sufi shrines in Timbuktu, Mali. The militant group, known as Ansar Dine (Defenders of Faith), attacked the city's ancient mosques and mausoleums associated with local Sufis, arguing that shrine worshipping is offensive to Shariah. "Shrines are haram. We will destroy them all, without exception," said the group. The assault on Sufi shrines alarmed the world. The United Nations placed Timbuktu mosques on the List of World Heritage in Danger. The faith-filled violence against the concept and artifacts of Sufi spirituality reignites a broader question whether Sufi spirituality is compatible with Shariah. Small-minded versions of Islam emanating from pedestrian groups within the Muslim world undermine Sufi Spirituality that forges alliances among diverse religions and denominations to lead human species to a common and universal spirituality.

Over the centuries, the Orientalists (a breed of Western scholars who studied Islamic history and culture in the period of colonialism) have been censorious of Shariah but appreciative of Sufism. The dichotomy continues. In nurturing this dichotomy, some Western scholars are anti-Shariah, some are unacquainted with Islam; some are motivated to moderate what they perceive as the "excesses of Shariah", such as persecution of religious minorities, subjugation of women, and imposition of harsh criminal punishments. Unfortunately, scholars bereft of mysticism are incapable of understanding the Sufi ways because intellectualized scholarship can barely see beyond the walls of argumentation.

Muslim Sufis strive to expand law's space for tolerance, egalitarianism, and spiritual diversity. However, no version of Sufism can discard Shariah without undermining Islamic law. Lawless Sufism does little to improve a satisfying way of life for most Muslims. Law is indispensable for the construction and maintenance of an ordered society. Equally true, however, is the fact that law without enlightened criticism leads to cruelty. Contemporary opposition to Shariah in the West and denunciation of Sufism in some Muslim communities, both are misguided.

Sufis are made differently from jurists and judges. There are no schools or universities that offer certificates or degrees to become Sufis. It requires years of education and professional knowledge for a person to be a jurist, judge, or learned person. Shariah judges and jurists acquire special knowledge after years of studying the Qur'an, the Prophet's Sunnah, the fiqh, and Islamic secular law found in modern constitutions, legislation, and treaties. By contrast, Sufis may or may not begin as scholars of law. Sufis are cultivated in the veiled folds of knowledge, mystery, intuition, worship, wanderings, and purity. The Sufi seeks, and eventually lives in, a world free of ego, greed, gluttony, intemperance, ingratitude, envy, jealousy, lust, demons, kings, queens, and fools.

Much like ordinary Muslims, Sufis subscribe to the five obligations of Shariah. The Shariah mandates that Muslims believe in One God and in the prophecy of Muhammad, say the daily five prayers, fast in the month of Ramadhan, give zakat (charity), and perform the hajj (pilgrimage) if they can afford it. Sufis discharge these five obligations day and night. In fact, most Sufis do more than minimal observance of the five obligations. They say optional prayers throughout the day, fast throughout the year, and generously give charity. Every moment of their life is devoted to the remembrance of God. They pray during the day and during the night, give charity openly and secretly, remember God boisterously and wordlessly, and send salutations to all Prophets by their tongues and hearts.

Since the introduction of Islam in the seventh century, the province of Khorasan has been the most cherished homeland for Sufis. Khorasan (comprised of numerous cities including Nishapur, Balkh, Ghazni, Merv, Samarkand, and Bukhara) nurtured great hadith-collectors, scientists, jurists, and Sufis of Islam. The seventh-century Iraq, when its cultural identity was Mesopotamian more than Arab, was a favorite abode of master Sufis. Najaf, an Iraqi town where Imam Ali Ibn Abu Talib is buried, excels in Sufi spirituality.

Sufis have always lived, openly and secretly, in cities and villages of Egypt. Fallen to militarism, modern Egyptians appear to have drifted away from Sufi spirituality. Morocco, particularly the city of Fez, is blessed with the Sufi heritage, opening the way for West African Muslims to experience the raptures of mysticism. Pakistan and India remain most hospitable to Sufi spirituality as the people in this region seek to reconcile various religious traditions.

Unfortunately, Muslims are divided over Sufi spirituality. Some misguided governments and clerical organizations are anti-Sufi. For the most part, however, Muslim communities respond kindly to Sufi spirituality. Muslims in Turkey, Indonesia, Malaysia, Pakistan, Afghanistan, and India are wide open to the teachings of Sufis. Muslims in these countries see no contradiction between Islamic law and Sufi spirituality.

By contrast, Saudi Arabia, United Arab Emirates, and some other Gulf mini-states have little reverence for Sufi spirituality and see Islamic mysticism as a threat to the integrity of Islam. Many governments are suspicious of Sufis because Sufis are unlikely to support royal families, kingships, and other forms of power that elevate some families over others. Despite official hostility to Sufi spirituality in some countries, Sufis in all Muslim nations continue to influence individuals, families, towns, and communities.

Sufi spirituality is not a separate sect of Islam. Nor is Sufi spirituality more aligned with the Shia or the Sunni sect. While Iranian culture and sensibilities have greatly influenced the construction and development of mysticism, Sufi spirituality is not a branch of Shia theology. Most prominent Sufis have been raised with the Sunni faith. More recently, the Wahhabis have been vociferously opposed to Sufi spirituality. Many attacks on Sufi shrines are inspired by the theology of Wahhabism. In a protracted contest, however, generous Sufi spirituality will likely win over narrow-minded sectarianism.

30. UNIVERSAL MATING

Universal mating is interweaving a bold new humanity of countless features and complexions. This trend, most powerful in the United States, is not the culmination of the 1960s hippie movement but captures the ever-present human will to mate and produce children across racial, ethnic, color, and geographical barriers. Despite the earlier laws forbidding interracial marriages, American blacks and whites have been procreating "mixed" children ever since the two people came together in the original colonies. Almost from the beginning, the newcomers, blacks and whites, mated with Native Americans and indigenous Mexicans to produce interracial children. Unfortunately, many interracial children were born out of forced sexual relations.

Gradually, interracial procreation became more consensual and complex. U.S. immigration was opened to Eastern Europeans, Asians, Arabs, South Indians, Iranians, and Central Asians, creating a microcosm of the world. Now the individuals of diverse races, ethnicities, colors, and physiologies are coming together in ever larger numbers to launch a new generation of Americans who cannot be confined to prior racial, ethnic, and color categories. This fusion across conventional racial borders is a budding sign of universal mating -- something other nations will inevitably follow -- as it weakens the age-old obsessions with imagined racial purity and color.

Universal Mating

Universal mating is a profound principle of natural law. It illuminates the essence of human species. It celebrates the diversity of human features and complexions. In fact, nature endows each and every individual with unique features and a special hue and brightness of complexion. Rarely do any two individuals look exactly the same; such are nature's open secrets. Universal mating recognizes that all features and complexions are inherently exquisite, and that no racial or color mixing is more attractive for producing children. All children are precious not because they all are the same underneath differing features and pigments but because they all are different in their appearances. An infinite variety in the subtle colors of human skin is nature's immutable promise.

As a matter of principle, personal preferences rather than social models determine the dynamics of universal mating. Who mates with whom is an interpersonal decision; it is no longer a matter over which parents, neighbors, or pundits need to worry. Laws and regulations, secular or clerical, which prohibit procreation on the basis of race or color are void ab initio, contrary to the natural law of universal mating. Social taboos that snare individuals into castes, prohibiting inter-caste procreation, are spirituality bankrupt. Consensual mating free of social fears is divine, carrying out the sacred plan of human survival and evolution.

Procreation

Procreation is the sine qua non of universal mating,

even though many loving partners cannot produce children. Having sex with a person of different race or color without the intention of producing a child can be love, romance, promiscuity, adventure, and social rebellion. There is nothing wrong with non-procreative sexual activity. But consensual mating for procreative purposes is the most credible contribution to the fusion of humanity, and it does not matter whether the partners are attracted to each other for love, money, social status, or some other material benefits.

At the present stage of human civilization, universal mating summons the courage to defy the prohibitive philosophies of racial barriers, caste separations, and color hierarchies. Interracial procreation is an act of courage in apartheid and racist societies. It is mission impossible in caste-bound communities. Like all things that challenge deeply seated conventions, universal mating is far from popular. Persons opting for universal mating may be condemned as social outcasts, rebels, and misfits.

Obstacles

While the United States, because of its relatively wider immigration policy, is a country most conducive to the cultivation of universal mating, the rest of the world is still confined to the paradigm of racial and ethnic homogeneity. The global population layout is highly segregated. Africa is predominantly black; Europe is predominantly white; China and India, the most populous countries of the world, have few Europeans or Africans. In India the caste system further rigidifies matrimonial barricades. The Middle East has a huge population of foreign workers, but cultural and religious taboos discourage interracial marriages.

The cyberspace allows matrimonial websites to bring together individuals of diverse cultures, colors, and national origins, but only few cyber romances turn into fruitful mating. Physical distance, expensive traveling, and visa restrictions are significant obstacles against finding mates in other countries.

While the peoples in other countries wait for a promising but uncertain future when they will be free to find mates anywhere in the world, the people in the United States have begun a remarkable phenomenon of the fusion of races, ethnicities, and colors. "America the beautiful" is in the process of adding a new layer to its meaning.

31. CRUELTY PRODUCES HATRED

Revulsion is a strong human emotion deeply wired in our sense of justice. We develop feelings of revulsion against individuals, groups, even nations that perpetrate gross injustice and cruelty. In an increasingly integrated world, the information travels with the speed of light in all corners of the planet, often in real time. The peoples of the world develop instant feelings of aversion against entities that commit crimes against humanity, erase homes and villages, and kill powerless men, women, and children with rockets and missiles. A well-resourced entity may win a battle or a war, and yet may sow disgust in the hearts of the peoples of the world. Cruelty may go unpunished in the national and international legal systems but it cannot escape the realm of human awareness.

For surely, we know, cruelty breeds odium - a permanent decree of nature. The decree cannot be annulled with any teachings of law or morality. Nor can the decree be circumvented through false propaganda, news distortions, or legalistic arguments touting self-defense or national security in the commission of brutality.

There is no defense for cruelty. Nor is there any exception that allows cruelty. "Love your enemies and pray for those who persecute you" is a noble command. In the imperfect world, however, "cruelty breeds odium" is a more readily observable phenomenon.

Acts of Cruelty

Unfortunately, current national and global affairs are replete with acts of cruelty. Individual acts of cruelty disturb us profoundly, all of us, even when we do not know the victims or the wrongdoers. The peoples of the world, no matter where they live, are revolted when they hear a man raping an eight year old girl, breaking her bones and smashing her face with a hammer, a mother shooting her four children eighteen times at close range, or a young man massacring twenty children in an elementary school. For many, even acts of cruelty against animals are reprehensible. We may recognize that some individual acts of cruelty stem from mental illness or psychotic disorder. Yet, we do not love cruel persons.

Acts of cruelty associated with groups and nations produce even more intense revulsion. The peoples of the world rightfully presume that groups and nations act deliberately in committing torture and cruelty. Waterboarding an enemy does not occur accidentally, though bombing a wedding party might be a targeting mistake. Ethnic cleansing is a deliberate act of cruelty, as is genocide and forcible removal of an indigenous population. Recurrent bombing of hospitals, places of worship, shops, emergency vehicles, and similar targets, even when arguably excusable under the law of war, produce odium and feelings of revulsion. Such is the law of nature that the peoples of the world hate all forms of cruelty. No excuse or justification mitigates the feelings of revulsion against cruelty.

Expressions of Hatred

The peoples of the world express odium against cruelty in many different ways. The direct victims of cruelty, though weak and powerless, may resort to violence and sabotage, at times inviting more cruelty. They may supplicate deities for heavenly retribution. When cruelty subsides, the victims may build memorials and write stories and poems to express their disgust.

The feelings of odium are most intense when cruelty is committed in the context of alien domination, occupation, and apartheid. When the peoples of the world see or learn about cruelty, they, though not directly affected by it, may protest loudly and quietly. The peoples of the world may burn effigies of the leaders of cruelty. They may boycott products and urge for broader divestment in companies doing business with unkind entities.

The perpetrators of cruelty jeopardize their own safety. As reaction to cruelty, the revulsion is sometimes so fervent and widespread that it reaches even the blameless members of the entity. Collective punishment solicits collective revulsion. Just as cruelty sees no distinction among its victims, likewise the reactive odium turns blind. This is the most unfortunate logic of cruelty.

Frequently, memories of cruelty are intergenerational, as stories of cruelty travel in time and space. Such is the law of nature that the battles won with cruelty are eventually written off. History is revised. And the posterity is ashamed of their cruel forefathers. Self-loathing is the ultimate price of engaging in cruelty.

ABOUT THE AUTHOR

L. Ali Khan initially trained as a civil engineer. He later switched to law, obtaining a law degree from Punjab University, Lahore. In 1976, Khan immigrated to the United States and studied law at New York University School of Law where he received his LL.M. and J.S.D. Khan is a member of the New York Bar.

In 2014, Khan founded Legal Scholar Academy to provide social, political and foreign policy assessments to Muslim nations and communities. Khan's commentaries are available on iTunes, Daily Motion, and YouTube.

Khan has authored several books, including *The Extinction of Nation-States* (1996), *A Theory of Universal Democracy* (2003), *A Theory of International Terrorism* (2006), and *Contemporary Ijtihad: Limits and Controversies* (2011), *Islam Enters America* (2015).

Over the years, Khan has written numerous academic articles and essays on Islamic law, international law, commercial law, creative writing, legal humor, jurisprudence, the U.S. Constitution, comparative constitutional law, human rights, and foreign policy. His academic writings are used as part of course materials in universities across the world.

www.ingramcontent.com/pod-product-compliance
Lightning Source LLC
Chambersburg PA
CBHW070426290526
45791CB00005B/1854